Unscripted: How Women Thrive in Life, Business, and Relationships

Real Life Advice from Women on Balancing Their Power

Unscripted: How Women Thrive in Life, Business, and Relationships, Real Life Advice from Women on Balancing Their Power Complied and Published by Ann M. Evanston, San Pablo, CA

www.unscriptedstories.com

Copyright © 2018 Ann M. Evanston

ISBN 9781982907891

Independently Printed

Cover design by Kerry Hargraves
Cover photograph by Levi Guzman on Unsplash.com

Contents

Prologue from the Creator of Unscripted: Ann M. Evanston

I remember the day I had the vision to create the Unscripted series. It was beautiful and sunny in the San Francisco bay area. Sitting in my huge organic garden as the sounds of birds chirped and bees hummed, I was reflecting. I had spent the last three days teaching a small group of high level corporate leaders how to draw upon stories in their lives to influence and inspire others. As a woman who truly believes in the power of stories and had worked coaching individuals for years on how to draw from their own lives to teach, inspire and heal others, bringing a group together to do this work nourished my soul.

Feeling the warm sun on my face, watching our vegetables grow, I had a simple vision: I must bring more stories of people everywhere to life. I have tried in other ways before. Ordinary Extraordinary Women was just one example. Then, I was TOO in control... wanted things "my way." What, an alpha female wanting to be in control? Lol, but it can get in the way of our greatest good!

I learned and let go and realized that I wanted the storytellers to be in control. I would manifest the broad category. THEY decide what story and lesson to share with readers. Too many other story books control all the factors: the type of story, the writing format or style, even the moral. Those books are great, but the stories often feel like one person could have written them all. *What if the stories were in each person's unique voice?*

I connected with a girlfriend that always delights in my journey like your best friend did when you were six. Remember that friend that thought everything about you was awesomesauce? She lives life that way as a grown ass woman! Her eyes glittered with energy at the idea. She asked: "Will you select the main topics for the storytellers to choose from for submission to each eBook?"

My heart opened wide: "No," I responded. "I want the universe to attract them and the story they want to tell. Once I have enough stories submitted I see myself printing them all (I know, it's an eBook!) and seeing what emerges, selecting those main topics as I read them as a collection."

"Ohhhh…!" she said. "I love that idea."

"Then I can write a 'prologue' if you will, for each section. Possibly telling my own story."

Unscripted Stories was born. I selected two eBooks to start. More eBooks in the series keep manifesting. I reached out to friends, colleagues and on social media. I emailed my lists. Those who hearts were an easy yes have shown up to share. Each writer was called to be a part.

Our stories inspire. They heal. And transform. I am moved by the raw vulnerability of each storyteller. I revel in their unique story telling style. Stories. Told though generations, cultures, companies and friends. We tell stories to connect with others, to teach lessons learned, to motivate and move change.

We seek stories to show us we are not alone They inspire us to live our best lives. To heal parts of ourselves. To realize we are not alone on our journey.

I took several weeks to read the 41 stories that have created this eBook: *"Unscripted: How Women Thrive in Life, Business, and Relationships (Real life advice from Women on Balancing their Power),"* I transformed. Women wrote about everything and nothing I expected. And EVERY story is mesmerizing, vulnerable and real. Some made me chuckle. Others filled my heart with sadness. Many had lessons for me and others inspired me. *My wish is that they do the same for you.*

The five "themes" of this eBook emerged after reading every story. They manifested organically as I read. As I look at them, they are all so critical to thriving!

Most importantly as I read? I know I am not alone. As women, what creates our power isn't something outside of us. It is 100% in our control. And the journey to discovering that makes us thrive. Our paths aren't the same and the lessons are learned at different stages in life. But when you are ready to learn them? The story unfolds.

Each writer has graciously given contact info, some even further resources. Connect. Share. Be a part of this amazing community. Join our Facebook Community: https://www.facebook.com/groups/unscriptedstories/ and interact with more amazing people in the community!

There are several things that make these eBooks special:

Each story is written in the author's own voice. They were not forced to write into a format or follow a specific writing style. As you read you will see the uniqueness, flair, and energy of everyone.

I allowed every author to choose the story they were called to share. All that guided them was the title. I firmly believe that the universe decided what was important to share with you.

In addition, they chose what they want to take from their story, a lesson if you will. As I read them, there is SO MUCH more one can learn and take away.

Once all stories were submitted, I tapped into the heart of each and found that "themes" emerged. At the beginning of each section I share further, even with my own stories.

This is a great book to simply turn to the table of contents, close your eyes, point and read ANY story…it probably called you! Of course, you can also think about the themes and your own personal journey as well.

Read with your heart, think about your life. Be inspired. Take a step. Laugh. Maybe shed a tear or two as you think about YOU in their stories. I would also love if you share how a story impacted your life!

I also invite you to Become an Author in another eBook in the Unscripted series, your stories matter! http://www.unscriptedstories.com/become-an-author/

Welcome to Unscripted: How Women Thrive in Life, Business, and Relationships (Real life advice from Women on Balancing their Power)!

About the Creator, Ann M. Evanston

Stories are a fabric in my life. From as far back as I can remember, amazing stories with beautiful lessons we're always told. From "The Giving Tree" to "The Velveteen Rabbit", as a little girl I knew stories had value.

Even as a teenager reading stories was sometimes an escape from my life, and also recognition of what I was going through. Judy Blume made me laugh and cry all at the same time!

Something interesting happens in adult life more often than not: reading stories ends. Or more accurately the only stories we see on the news. And those stories aren't my favorite!

My career has been about people knowing and owning their stories. Being an expert in influence, personal power, and self-worth, I have always utilized clients story to show them who they are. Teaching how to tell a personal story to create buy in and influence others. Rewriting your own stories to step into your power and truly know and are excellent. And understanding how self-worth is an internal process and your story has led you to greatness.

All stories, no matter how big or small can have a powerful impact on me, you, and others around us. Sometimes we don't even know how our stories are touching or impacting people.

Because my expertise is transforming lives, I wanted to bring together a series of books that would demonstrate and support others. Unscripted stories will do just that.

Oh, you want all the official biography stuff?

Ann M. Evanston, MA, a world-renowned speaker, consultant and trainer, has over 25 years of experience in the field of influence, personal power, and inspired leadership, and is the founder of three organizations that are still running today.

She has consulted extensively with clients including Cisco, Stanford Medical Center and Clinics, Sutter Health Network, Redding Rancheria Tribal Organization, Teichert Aggregates Construction, and Strategies to Empower People.

Ann has traveled nationally for over 20 years delivering workshops, retreat and keynotes on Building Your Influential Voice, Women's Empowerment, art of facilitating and true leadership. In 2001, she had the honor of presenting "Don't Sweat the Small Stuff," by Dr. Richard Carlson across the U.S.

With a passion for speaking that was ignited in the seventh grade when she participated in toastmasters, she is now working with groups ranging from 20 to 5000. She has spoken on stages with the Reverend Jesse Jackson, Dr. Richard Carlson, Tory Johnson, and Loral Langemeier to name a few.

Ann's expertise in leadership development began with her own experience as a manager. Her first position was leading volunteers for Jump Start, a now nationally modeled program she developed. As Assistant Director she was responsible for a team of nine, and as Executive Director a team of forty-eight.

Understanding how to step into your personal power, know your legacy as a great leader and develop others, especially women, to live their lives on fire is her life's purpose. Ann is a published author of: *The Influence Factor: The Journey to Discovering Your Influential Voice,* and co-authored: *The Power of Leadership Producing Results*/Feb. 2009; and *The Power of Leadership in Business Networking*/Aug. 2009.

Ann was named a top 6 leadership consultant by About.com in 2011. She holds a B.A. in Sociology from Whitman College and an M.A. in Psychology from Antioch University Seattle. She is a DDI certified facilitator and Certified Behavioral Technology facilitator.

Section 1 - Who am I

Finding ME....Again: by Ann Evanston

Who am I? The internal question. Who am I? No really. Who the hell am I?

I am asking myself AGAIN.

I first wrote that 3 word question for others to ponder in my book published in 2012: *"The Influence Factor: The Journey to Discovering Your Influential Voice."* Self-discovery leads to owning our own voice, speaking up with confidence, letting go of false perceptions. It ultimately allows us to BE regardless of roles, titles and responsibilities. With knowing ourselves we let go of what everyone else thinks.

Knowing myself is still a journey of self-discovery. In my work with women and building self- esteem, I choose to role model pressing deeper and deeper into ME. To see more of me. Understand me. Be me. As do each of us.

I recall one time, yes this happens more than once in our lives, when I realized that I was not serving my best self. I was contracting as a seminar speaker (I started toastmasters in 7th grade and love speaking and facilitation), traveling the globe teaching topics to groups in hotels around the world. It seemed like a perfect way for me to share my knowledge, tell stories and inspire others to live their best lives.

Back then, most speakers were men. I managed to find myself in a very elite, top rated group of speakers who gave amazing seminars but also sold books and tapes for personal development beyond the one-day seminar. Being a part of this 1% AND the only woman at that time, opened further doors for me. The contract opportunities came in. Before you know it, I was living the "roller board lifestyle" – pack the carryon suitcase on Saturday, fly out Sunday. Different city every day, only to fly home late Friday night and do it again. And the seminar company was BRILLANT at the psychology of acknowledgment: voice mails to the speakers about my successes; asked to speak at the speakers' conference, awards, applause, accolades....better trips!

Earl, my amazing life partner, was extremely supportive. If it was what I wanted, he wanted me to be happy. No one can ask for anything better. So, I pushed forward on this journey.

One night, about two years into this schedule, I distinctly remember flying home. I left Denver late to return home, and the flight, as is often true in the winter, was delayed. I always tried to use my airline status to upgrade, but not this evening, so I used my priority seating to get a window seat. It was almost midnight on Friday as we heard the pilot say we are starting our descent.

Flying into the San Francisco bay was beautiful. It was a clear, and cold (for us, lol) night. Golden light shone brightly all over the bay. The water created huge black voids from the south, north. I could see the Dumbarton Bridge, then the San Mateo Bridge across those voids, like veins pulsing life. Cars traveling west and east pumping the energy of the bay. Off in the distance I could see the amazing skyline of San Francisco, the heart of the area.

Looking out the tiny portal I started to weep. I fell in love with the bay area during a choir trip in college and when Earl asked me to move there to be with him, I did. I LOVE it there. I LOVED him, I LOVED life there.

And I was NEVER home.

"Who are you Ann?" A tiny voice whispered in my heart as I looked out the portal and wiped the tears away. "What really matters?"

That weekend I shared that I needed to create a six-month plan to leave the contractual relationship with the seminar company behind and live MY life.

I have never regretted that decision. I am still a speaker and a facilitator. But that is WHAT I DO. Not who I am. I was losing myself in what everyone else thought. Being more me each and every day makes life enjoyable. I learned that I cannot buy into what others think my "best life" is. Only I know who she is.

Now, teaching women how to find "her", and love "her" is my mission. The joy that pours though me is the best feeling ever! I invite you to learn more about my Women's Self-Love Evolution Retreat. In addition, grab the free e-version of my book *The Influence Factor*. I have a wonderful "Who am I" activity in the book for you!

As you read each woman's "who am I" story, you will see this journey of having to find "her" at different moments, events and situations. We must know "who am I" spiritually, emotionally, and yes, even sexually! Knowing the answer to "who am I" allow you to find your authentic voice and speak it beautifully!

About Ann M Evanston

Whether you are a woman wanting the confidence to be seen in your work, or to get the promotion, or you're a woman who aspires to be valued in your relationships or to grow your own business... Ann M. Evanston, MA has the system that delivers results. Her focus is on YOUR success through building influence, personal power and self-worth. She has been featured on The Huffington Post, Spark and Hustle with Tory Johnson, and Showcasing Women, and has spoken on stages globally. About.com named her one of the "Top 6" Marketing consultants. She is a published author of: _"The Influence Factor: The Journey to Discovering your Influential Voice."

Mom's Effigy
by Sherry Prindle

"Your mom is mean."

"Mean? What are you talking about?"

This was the first time my boyfriend was meeting Mom, and the first time I had heard anyone say something like that about her. Wondering what brought him to that conclusion, I let the comment go.

Mom was famous for being generous, so I smiled that night when she insisted on treating us to a Texas dinner at the Trail Dust Steakhouse. She alerted the server that she was paying, but at the end of the meal, my boyfriend motioned for the check. When the server brought it to him, my mom grabbed her wrist, saying, "I told you I was getting the check." That was quite embarrassing – and mean.

I tried to think of things she may have done when I was a child that would be considered mean but came up blank. It was just what I considered normal, and I never saw her as mean before the wrist-grabbing incident.

After that, though, there was plenty to notice:

"Why don't you just get a regular job; who would want to travel like you do all the time."

"That outfit looks horrible. I don't know why anyone would wear those colors."

"Why do you bring that 9-layer dip over here; no one likes it."

She "teased" perfect strangers in awkward ways, like at the express checkout counter: "What are you doing with 11 items? Didn't you read the sign…just joking…"

I also started noticing things people said about me: "There you go again, why do you have to be so critical?"

The characteristics in me that resembled Mom contributed to the Texas relationship ending, so I moved back to Missouri. Mom was living with my cousins, where there was a constant parade of their children and grandchildren. Mom would shoo the young ones out of her room screeching, "Go on, get out of here. I don't want you kids in here breaking things."

My cousins called me regularly with reports of insults and shenanigans like stuffing her clothes into cracks and under doors, not to keep out the cold, but because she said, "I saw a mouse run across my floor. And it's no wonder; with all the clutter in the dining room."

I would apologize and offer to stop traveling so I could take her off their hands, but they would say, "No, we love Aunt Mary; she's hilarious." Hilarious?

I loved hanging out at my cousins', cooking dinner and playing Texas Hold 'em. When I stayed late, Mom would come out of her room to say, "Sherry, it's almost 11 o'clock. Shouldn't you be going home?" "Mom, I'm 40 years old!" I would say as my cousins laughed uproariously.

On an East Coast road trip, it became clear that this "mean mom" thing was not something that appeared after I became an adult. We weren't sure where to go from Philadelphia, and I asked how she felt about Atlantic City. She said she didn't care. When we got there, though, she didn't want to gamble or walk on the beach or shop along the boardwalk. She was surly and said she didn't want to go to Atlantic City in the first place, blaming me for ruining the vacation by taking her there. I felt a familiar powerlessness and sobbed like a 6-year-old, saying, "But you said you didn't care!"

She watched a lot of TV, and I noticed her big-screen was blurry. She insisted it was fine and was furious when I bought her a new one. She went on and on in that witchy voice about how she told me she didn't need it and that she "hated my guts." I was beside myself feeling upset, tears rolling down my cheeks. As I took the old TV out to the curb, my cousin's husband laughed, "She keeps insisting she didn't need a TV. We got her a space heater she refuses to use too. It gets below 40 degrees in there, but she won't budge." He was having a great time recounting the idiocy of my mom's antics. I listened, horrified, and looked at how he enjoyed these stories.

At that moment, it occurred to me. They are experiencing the same person I am. They observe the same behavior, endure the same abuse, and hear the same tone. But they find it hilarious . . . and so could I.

I chose to look at the things my mother did as funny. When it got late while we played cards, my cousins would call out, "Aunt Mary, it's 11 o'clock, and Sherry's still here," as I laughed. When she insulted my weight, career, cooking, or choice of gifts, I grinned and said, "thanks, Mom."

How she was didn't have to affect how I was. And how others treat you doesn't determine how you feel. In corporate training on Managing Emotions and Dealing with Difficult People, I coach from my personal experience to view situations like you would a TV Sitcom. Examine something you feel negatively about and choose to see it as humorous.

When Mom passed, I was privileged to sing at her funeral and remember her fondly with no resentment.

The next time I went camping with my cousins, I brought Mom's red canvas chair. Everyone lined fold-up chairs around the campfire. Mom was the only one who had always insisted, "Stay out of my chair," so I took delight in setting it up and announcing that anyone who wanted could now sit in that chair. We had fun with that premise the entire weekend. On the last night while everyone was away from the fire preparing to cook dinner, a strange gust of wind picked up only my mom's chair and whisked it into the fire. I called everyone to look. As we watched this vestige of my mom's presence at previous camping trips being consumed by the flames, in cathartic release, I called out in a cackling witch voice:

"I told you not to sit in my chair!"

About Sherry Prindle

International speaker and corporate trainer, Sherry Prindle has delivered over 3,000 presentations in three languages. She founded the Professional Coach Academy where she has been instrumental in launching the careers of over 1,200 professional speakers and coaches.

Author of Women of Influence, she organizes the biannual Star Marketing Summit and hosts a radio show for entrepreneurs. Sherry has an M.A. in Business and Linguistics

She speaks Japanese and Russian, having lived in both countries. She enjoys traveling, camping, singing, trail running, and team trivia.

Contact Sherry to spark long-term change in your personal or professional life, visit http://sherryprindle.com

Get past emotional situations and gain control with Emotional Effigy: The Power to Replace Negativity Activity Book at www.SherryPrindle.com/Effigy

Self-Acceptance Leads to Power
by Mimi Meadows

I grew up in a violent alcoholic home. Violence that began in my infancy. I honestly don't know how I survived. How violent? Well, neck, back and especially, PTSD problems do abound. I was a recipient of my mother's self-hatred and I became a practitioner. I didn't like myself, so why would anyone else. This pain didn't allow me to trust others or myself. The 'myself' part would turn into a-not-listening to myself or my needs and wants kind of lifestyle. I spent way too much time in my head obsessing over everyone else's needs and wants and solving their problems. My heart would pound during conflict even if I wasn't involved. It was a terrifying and despairing time in my life. At a young age I regularly wished for death. I feared and hated my mother and step-father. My biological father's complete absence was a quiet knife that lodged itself deep in the back ground of my heart. It daily reminded me and silently solidified my worthlessness.

I grew up in an atmosphere where not asking for what I wanted or needed was rewarded. This made me a tough and good kid in my parent's eyes and I desperately needed some kind of affirmation even it was a sick one. Still, I was no one's precious little angel in that house. Nurture? What the hell was that? Are you kidding me? I was the little brown whipping 'thing'. My needs and wants took backseat to everyone else in the house, but most of the time, no seat. As harsh as it was, it was all I knew. It was 'my normal'.

You might imagine how this home affected me, laying the toxic ground from which I sprung. Copious amounts of insecurity coupled chronic codependent behavior and thinking. I hated my mother and everything about her. I suppose I rebelled, quietly inside, cause out loud I would have got an awful beating on my bare ass with a leather belt. My childhood mantra was 'whatever mom does, do the opposite.' With all I could muster I tried to be a 'good girl'. I nearly gave up the age of 12 when my mother had a mental breakdown. Yea! The men in white came and took her away. Fucking foster home! I really felt old and wanted to die then. Utter despair. I almost gave up! The day after I had decided to give up, my brother and I were sent home. My excitement crushed when upon arrival I received an ass chewing from my mom on how I needed to do more around the house so that it doesn't happen again.

At sixteen I had a spiritual awakening, definite God moment. It opened my eyes to a new way of thinking, living, and being. At the beginning of this spiritual journey I felt that heavy backpack of hatred and anger drop off. I began to have joy like I never knew. Little steps here and there of hope and healing. Since that awakening in '84 bits and pieces of my childhood keep falling off revealing a beautiful person. I am still on that journey. I try every day to consciously make contact with God. I do believe in miracles and I cannot emphasize how important that has been and still is for me. I try every day to quiet my mind and seek God.

A number of decades have past and living in mental/emotional health isn't anything I have mastered. It's a practice. I have a fantastic therapist! Nothing wrong with professional help. I may not do everything right, but I am doing better. At times PTSD rears its head. Sometimes, I have panic attacks. These I do not ignore. I treat myself with kid gloves. I am gentle and patient. I deserve a little loving. I take lots of naps. My physical health has suffered much from Adverse Childhood Effect, yeah, that's a thing. Gentleness and patience with my healing have not been easy. My head really thinks I should be "over" all this. What a fantasy!

Today most of my pain comes when I still hold on to people, places, and things. When I am fatigued or sick and I'm trying to do too much. AGAIN! When I find myself trying to control, manage, and manipulate situations or others, I am in a bad place. All of which, I have no control. I find peace and joy in letting go…or be dragged, yea!

I have learned that if I can't love and accept myself, I can't love and accept others. Loving myself is setting boundaries with others. NO, is a complete sentence. I have learned to be gentle to myself. I have learned to listen to my body. I have limits. I have learned self-care. Self-care is being myself, not what I think others want or need me to be. It is NOT negotiable. When I practice this, it becomes easier and easier to stop hiding and be who I am.

Loving myself is a journey and a living, growing thing. It bubbles and brews out all over the place! Am I perfect? Hell no! There are still bad days, but not as many as there used to be. Now that I have compassion, patience, and understanding for myself, it flows out more and more to others without me saying a word! It's turning me into the kind of person I want to be around. Acceptance and love are irresistible. That's power! It allows others to rest and be themselves. It puts them at ease, allowing for creativity and honesty. I mean SERIOUSLY? Who DOESN'T wanna be around that?

As women we often hit roadblocks in life because we don't understand our past and its effects. These must be lovingly and patiently dealt with if we want success in our relationships. You must start with yourself first.

About Mimi Meadows

Mimi Meadows lives in northwest Washington where she is surrounded by her loving husband, a teddy bear of a man since 1987, two adult children and three pets. She has worn many hats from teacher, office administrator, mother, pastor's wife, baker, Zumba instructor, to musician and song writer. Currently, she is retired and thoroughly enjoys the empty nest that is her home. She continues to write and perform her own music as well as jazz and oldie covers locally under the stage name "Lady Mellow". She is a self-described unicorn because she is rare, mystical and has a built in "shive".

Contact info mimimeadows@live.com

Heeding the Call of the Void

by Stephenie Zamora

When I first heard the French phrase *"l'appel du vide,"* I was fascinated because it translates literally to *"the call of the void."* It's that common urge arising within perfectly sane and healthy individuals, who have no desire to die, *to leap off the edge of a cliff.* Have you felt it? I certainly have... it's even been studied!

I believe it's because nature activates something inside of us. For a moment, we experience the immensity of the world around us and we feel a desire to truly come alive. To feel limitless, expansive, and connected to something greater than ourselves. To break loose from the boxes that contain us, as well as the roles that confine us. *To fly free.* It's a strange and beautiful phenomenon that many people experience at some point in their lives, though it may feel different from person to person.

The concept of "the void" is one that's become intimately and passionately woven into my life over the last several years. The void is the inner gateway, the initiation, the path into deeper connection, peace, inspiration, love, purpose, intuition, and source — whatever those things mean for us individually. It's the layer between, just below the surface of day-to-day life. It's a magical, powerful, and sometimes terrifying place we all must visit at some point. That is, *if we want to truly step into who we're here to be and the work we're here to do. If we want to live a purposeful, passionate, deeply connected, and fully expressed life.*

My first experience with the void was entirely accidental. The memory of that moment is almost tangible for me, because it was a moment that changed the course of my life forever. I was living in Hawaii and had just gotten into a big fight with my then boyfriend. I went for a drive, looping around the island while sobbing endlessly.

I was so unhappy, depressed, and lost. I'd been fighting to "find myself" for *years* but wasn't getting anywhere. I felt like a failure and just wanted to give up. Parked at an overlook on the south end of Oahu, I sat in my car crying so hard I almost couldn't catch my breath. And that's when it happened.

I accidentally, *without any effort,* slipped and fell into the void. I moved through that pocket that felt like death, darkness, and emptiness — like I would simply disappear and never return — and moved immediately into a place of total peace.

Suddenly... I was calm.

It was almost like an out of body experience where I was still aware of myself sitting in the car at that overlook, yet my whole being, soul, and self felt like they were floating out amongst the Universe. I felt true peace, along with a clear sense that everything was just as it should be. More importantly, I had an unclouded connection to my *true self*... seeing and feeling who I was at my core in a way I never had before. It was this joyful, inspired, purposeful awareness that brought me to life in all the ways I'd craved, but could never cultivate.

Everything I'd been fighting and failing to create was alive inside me in that moment. I sat there, as time came to a halt, clinging to the experience for as long as I was able. And when it finally passed, I calmly drove myself home, bewildered by what had happened... but holding onto that vision and feeling as tightly as I could.

This experience of slipping and falling through the void changed everything. For the first time in my life, I had a clear sense of what it meant to have purpose. To know what I was working towards and who I was meant to become. It served as a guidepost that began pulling me forward, up and out of this depressed darkness that had held me hostage for most of my life.

Also, for the first time, I had a true sense that I was connected to something greater than myself. I had trust and faith in a benevolent Universe — some spirited, wise, all-knowing source or energy — and *knew* that everything was going to be okay if I just committed to closing the gap between where I was and what I'd felt inside that moment.

This experience repeated itself for many years. Every time I would reach the point I'd envisioned, I would have another experience of slipping and falling through the void, connecting with the next guidepost. It allowed me to *finally* create massive shifts in my life, work, and relationships... because I finally felt and understood what exactly I was working to create. I had a deeper level of knowing, beyond that of intellect, external "shoulds," and arbitrary goals.

This source, deep inside the void, allowed me to connect to my own intuitive wisdom, create more powerfully, and serve my audience in a deeper way. It allowed me to attract and connect with the most amazing tribe of friends, and I finally felt seen and appreciated for who I really was.

I began to blossom, built a thriving and successful business with a great team, and was finally doing the work I felt like I was here to do. Life was good. *So very, very good.* Until the end of 2014... when grief sucker punched me in the back of the head. When my very recent ex-boyfriend decided to take his own life as I vacationed with my family for the holidays, loss knocked the wind straight from my body and brought me to my knees. *Literally,* standing my mom's garage in the middle of the night while talking to a detective and trying not to wake up everyone up with my shocked, heartbroken tears.

As I learned to work with the grief, trauma, and PTSD, I uncovered many different healing modalities, and noticed that everything came back to that concept of the void... and from this place I've learned so much about what it means to truly *rise up* and *come back* from the darkest, hardest chapters of our lives.

The short: it requires a willingness to drop through the void – that pocket that feels like death, darkness, and emptiness... the unknown zone – in order to uncover the purpose of your path and cultivate a clear understanding and deep, wise knowing of what needs to happen next.

This is my invitation to you. No matter what you're going through, what path you're walking, where your time and attention are, or how frustrating and confusing things feel... *be willing to lean more deeply into the unknown.* To drop through "the void" despite all its terrifying uncertainty, so that you can move through to what comes next. Because it's only by going through it that you'll find what you're seeking... purpose, connection, trust, faith, joy, creativity, and peace. I promise you that.

About Stephenie Zamora

Stephenie Zamora is an author, life coach, business/marketing strategist, and founder of CallOfTheVoid.tv. Here she merges the worlds of personal development, energy healing, intuitive coaching, writing, and mixed media art to help individuals rise up and come back from the darkest, hardest chapters of life.

She guides her clients through the challenging process of re-orienting to their lives, relationships, and work in a way that's fully aligned with who they've become in the aftermath of loss, trauma, depression, and big life changes.

After struggling with PTSD, grief, and anxiety from a sudden and traumatic loss, she navigated her own difficult healing journey, and has set out to help others find the purpose of their own path. http://www.callofthevoid.tv

Are You Ready to Uncover the Purpose of Your Path? Download your personalized map for "rising up" and "coming back" from the darkest hardest chapters. Start creating a life, relationships, and business that's truly aligned with who you've become in the aftermath. http://www.callofthevoid.tv/the-heros-journey/

The Quest for Sexual Pleasure
by Stacy Michelle

For most of my adult life, my body felt like a foreign object that I was forced to inhabit. Starting at a young age, she felt so foreign to me that I would investigate her daily. Behind closed doors, I would look in a mirror and scrutinize every ounce of her. I was particularly focused on the size of my thighs and their "daily fluctuations". This sense of feeling like a stranger in my body was exacerbated by the fact that I never had a menstrual cycle like my teenage peers.

As I got older, I took refuge in my bright beautiful mind and one of the most linear professions on the planet, accounting. Right out of college, I got my CPA and began working in the Big Apple. On the outside, you would have seen a pretty young girl in black heels strutting up and down the streets of Manhattan. You may have pegged me for one of the characters on Sex in the City. On the inside, I felt like a character on the Freak Show. The ridicule of my body continued. As my girlfriends would talk about their orgasms and their ability to "rub one out", I sat in silence. Orgasm was an unknown concept to me. Even the infamous rabbit vibrator couldn't get me off. Yet another reason to add to the list of "Top 10 Reasons Why I Hate My Body".

Then came the moment of truth. I had a healing session which revealed that I had repressed childhood sexual trauma. It was like a bright light had illuminated the darkness inside of me. The hatred of my body, the inability to connect and feel safe within her. The absence of my menstrual cycle and my orgasm, it all made sense. In that moment, I knew I was given this information because it was time to heal. I set out on quest to reclaim my pleasure and come home to my body.

What makes a quest so epic are the challenges (e.g., monsters, booby traps) we need to overcome to claim our prize. My quest (which took the form of many healing sessions), required me to go on an archeological dig to find and feel the trauma. To feel the pain, fear, anger of not feeling safe and protected by my caregivers. Through that deep courageous journey, I found and rescued the little girl inside of me who was petrified of the world around her. I scooped her up in my loving arms and I let her know she was safe. I let her know that no one was ever going to hurt her ever again.

After I freed my inner child, the reclamation of my pleasure began. The body that had once been a place of scrutiny, had become a pleasure playground.

I became an avid student of Tantra and the Jade Egg. These practices made me come alive inside (pun intended). My sexual energy had awoken from a very deep slumber and she wasn't going back to sleep! I was basking in the glow of these practices so much that people would comment on how great I looked. I really wanted to tell them, it's because I am forming a deep connection to my pussy!

My quest to reclaim my pleasure reached a milestone while in Mexico on a tantric retreat where we would engage in hour long breath-work sessions. I was sprawled out naked on my yoga mat, one hand on my heart, the other hand on my womb. There was a cacophony of sounds all around me, some women were crying, some were yelling, and some were laughing. It was an epic symphony that no composer could recreate. As I breathed deeply in and out of my womb space, I shed tears of joy and my heart was full of love. I had come home to my body. She was there all along and it was in that moment that I felt safe enough to walk through the door and embrace her wholeheartedly.

The moral of the story is it is your divine birthright to go on an epic quest for pleasure in your body. To defeat the monsters and reclaim that which is rightfully yours, your sexuality, your sensuality, your joy, your love, your freedom of sexual expression. My hope is that after reading this you will feel inspired to go on this quest so in your own beautiful unique way.

About Stacy Michelle

I am a Speaker and Sexual Empowerment Coach to conscious women business owners around the world. When I am not supporting client with connecting to their bodies and their sexuality, you can find me salsa dancing, getting bendy on a yoga mat or hiking in beautiful British Columbia. I would love to have you join me on Facebook LIVE for Pleasure Talk Tuesday at 1pm PST here.

If you feel called to start you own pleasure quest, I am gifting you with a free 4-week video series entitled Awaken Your Orgasmic Potential: Four Keys to Sensational Sex which you can access here: http://bit.ly/2E0khBr

Believe My FemTruth – Breaking the Cycle of Misogynist Gaslighting

by Silvia Young

What is FemTruth? It's not for everyone. It's authenticity, it's sisterhood, it's courage. It's not something I was born with, but a wisdom you can embrace, a movement, a home.

I'll begin in the middle as it was the catalyst of enlightenment and revealed to me the ramifications of staying silent.

At 35 I was told I was infertile due to endometriosis. I had voiced my health concern since puberty, but was gaslit into believing I was misinformed, uneducated, and hysterical by each medical provider leading up to my final diagnosis. I let that happen to me.

I went to therapy to uncover how this exchange between a doctor and patient went so wrong. It was beyond infertility, it was now chronic health. Still being told it was psychosomatic when I was physically bedridden.

I learned that the female voice is repressed and oppressed. And not just in health. At first my rally cry was to end the social injustice of endometriosis (www.UniteEndo.org), but as I worked with my therapist, it became apparent that not having a voice in my own life was a constant. My new power is how I respond. Taking back my power means taking ownership of my life. I will never play the victim card. It's not me. I will not allow someone else that power over me.

So how did this begin?

It begins with my earliest memory being repeatedly thrown against a wall by a boy that was much bigger than myself. I was very young and scared, I was his personal rag doll to bully. I tried to speak up but was silenced, even with the visual bruising and emotional damage. My abuser was believed time and time again, over years. Believed by those I trusted to protect me. To this day, the gaslighting of my formative years continues, getting muddied with the added medical and professional abuse that transpired later.

Why didn't I speak louder?

It was the 70s, and then the 80s, and 90s.

Women's Rights advocates are demanding better, but in reality, it's still a fight to be believed in every facet of a female's life.

My last corporate job I was hired to run the Marketing Communications department. My challenge was to work with the "tech guys" developing the new platform I was preparing to launch. Silicon Valley is notorious for misogyny. But this was my career, not my health, not a personal scenario of abuse. In the workplace I was confident in my skills and had worked with many egos from all walks of life.

I lasted three tortuous months when I was humiliated at meetings, left out of big-picture discussions, and fighting for a place at the table. Each day felt like battle. After one meeting in particular, where the pure bass of said man's booming wrath was directed squarely on me, I folded.

I remember the feeling. I've had this feeling before. Silenced.

After that meeting I met with my boss, the CEO. He was compassionate in acknowledging the continued bullying and unprofessionalism said man vented on me and encouraged me to find a way to stroke said man's ego so that he would like me.

"When I want to have sex with my wife, I know I should wash the dishes and help put the kids to bed" said boss. "What changes can you make?"

I was not really understanding what he was asking of me but prepared to leave should one more incident arise. But I didn't need to. The next day I was fired for lacking to show leadership skills. He hoped I understood. (BTW … the company folded a few months later).

That had me thinking, has this silencing of my voice happened before in the workplace. Sure enough, I think back to my first job as a hostess for an upscale restaurant. The bartender, a married man more than 25 years my senior, would send me cocktails during work hours with seductive notes. He would conveniently be where I was, undressing me with his eyes and making sexual innuendos that made me uncomfortable.

Little did I know at the time that upon complaining, I would be scrutinized for bullying said bartender. Apparently, ignoring sexual innuendos and cocktails during work hours was confusing for said bartender when I was friendly with the other bartenders, servers and hostesses. So wait, everything was my fault? I complained about sexual harassment and it was my fault for somehow leading him on, or not responding positively? I was asked to be polite and smile. I later found out said bartender was the owner's cousin by marriage. I couldn't have been the first one to complain. I'm sure I wasn't the last. But I was silenced.

Or during my years at a PR agency when a male supervisor was caught bullying me on email. Leading up to the email I had complained about his behavior in meetings, and was gaslit, I was told I was being too sensitive "it couldn't be that bad" - then with proof, I was reprimanded. He was untouchable.

Too sensitive = gaslighting = silenced.

This pattern of being gaslit by men in power is misogyny. Not all men are misogynists. But, to the ones that are, I will not be silenced anymore to make you feel more powerful, more comfortable, more secure in your masculinity.

Because I am powerful in my FemTruth.

I want that empowerment for you, the reader. To reflect on your female journey and realize your own voice. Your truth. Your perspective as a female in a male-dominated world. And I want you to know something really important: When you are ready to stand in your FemTruth, unwilling to be silenced any longer, know that I will believe you.

About Silvia Young:

Silvia Young is an author, speaker, activist, and stage 4 endometriosis survivor. Her memoir *My FemTruth, Scandalous Survival Stories*, available on Amazon Kindle, is an inspiring journey – from bedridden in isolation to inspiring a FemTruth movement. She intimately shares how she overcame her most crushing decade after enduring twenty-five years of medical gaslighting and misdiagnoses due to an invisible illness, endometriosis. For more information go to www.SilviaYoung.com. Join the FemTruth Movement.

Accepting Loss and Developing Self Satisfaction
by Betty Root

After 32 years of marriage, it was difficult to accept the loss of my husband, Jim and move on to find self-satisfaction in life. I felt a void as Jim was my best friend, confidant and love of my life. Jim and I went through good and tough times together, supporting each other, and it was the first positive relationship of my life.

Growing up on a farm in Minnesota was a struggle as we did not have much money. I also had a difficult relationship with my mom as she would often make belittling remarks that that would make me feel stupid. Losing my father at the age of 17 made that relationship with my mom even more difficult. Ultimately, this drove me to make a life change. Leaving my family behind, I left home for California at the age of 20. The same year that I moved away, I married and fell into another relationship that did not serve me well. I worked and supported him financially while he attended college, but this support was not reciprocated when I tried to further my education/career. We had two children, but married life slowly became more of a struggle and increasingly stressful to the point that I had to make another life changing decision and end my marriage.

Two years later, I finally met the man that would change my life forever. Jim became my partner and best friend. He validated my feelings, helped me through some of my insecurities and encouraged my career. Sadly, it was a life together that was ultimately cut short by a disease.

In the final five years of Jim's life, I became his caregiver as he suffered from Lewy Bodies disease. As the disease progressed, I found myself taking on additional responsibilities -- chauffeur, cook, maid, security monitor, nurse -- the jobs increased as did the emotional and financial stress. Moving to Arizona alleviated some of the stress by having my oldest son live with us to help out. Nevertheless, I found myself increasing frustrated, short-tempered and exhausted. I was feeling guilty for having feelings of resentment towards the disease and also the loss of missed opportunities with this amazing man I loved.

After Jim's passing, I asked myself, "What now? How would I cope with the loss, the loneliness, and the feelings of what to do with my life now?" I had finally found stability with Jim, but now with him gone I found myself questioning my future. So much of my life had been wrapped up in his disease, and now I didn't know what I wanted to do.

Looking back at my life, health and fitness had always been a priority until my husband got sick. Looking at myself now I could see the toll of what taking care of Jim had done to me. Staring in the mirror, I could see how my body had changed and how stress had affected it. I realized I needed to make a change for myself, thinking, "This is where I would start! This is where I would begin my journey after Jim!"

I started going to a gym and working with a trainer who encouraged me. As I started to feel better, it took on new importance in my life. I found myself getting more excited about working out, and when my trainer suggested competing in a Body Building Show in the age 70 category, it gave me a new goal to achieve. Although it was exciting for a period of time, due to health issues and the pressure of constantly working out, I found myself pulling away from exercise.

This year I have again found myself at a crossroads in my life asking, "What do I want to accomplish?" Perhaps it sounds strange for someone in their 70s to talk about that – I've lived for seven decades after all -- but life doesn't stop after retirement or loss of a loved one. I now believe that I need more than just one thing to fill the emptiness that still overcomes me.

I've found a strong lifeline by talking with friends and family and sharing my daily encounters and feelings. This has been a way for me to embrace, understand and validate what I am going through. I find strength through God, and I pray for guidance and understanding as I look for my new path forward. Being surrounded by family also brings me joy and comfort. I'm fortunate to have my son and two grandsons nearby, and I visit my other grandkids often. Finally, keeping busy on a daily basis is cathartic, whether running errands, working in the garden or baking, I feel a sense of accomplishment. Does all of this provide me with enough self-satisfaction? Perhaps not, but it is a start.

I'm still looking for how to navigate my new life without Jim. It is still a work in progress for me. Writing this story to share has made me delve into my own relationship with myself, and I realize changes are important to bring closure to my empty feelings. My home is surrounded with memories of the past, but I am still working out how to incorporate change. Recently, after encouragement from a friend, I decided to paint and redesign my bedroom. A small change for sure, but another step forward for me.

This has made me realize that as I look back on my life, moments of change have had a real impact on the direction I have taken. Dealing with my husband's passing and then looking to find self-satisfaction in my life, the moments of change have been much smaller, they have been just as important in helping me identify who I am at 72 years of age and what I want to do with my life, and now I feel optimism towards the future.

Ultimately, if you have lost someone close to you it's important to reflect on the little things that create self-satisfaction. Never give up on living your life to the fullest.

About Betty Root

I grew up in Minnesota but spent most of my life in Northern California working at a community college and in the aerospace industry as a financial analyst. I raised two boys and was married to a college wrestling coach for 32 years until he passed away in 2015.

Since retiring, I studied massage and Ayurvedic healing, helped care for my autistic grandson, won a body building competition (age 70 category) and ziplined over Catalina Island in an attempt to keep myself feeling young. I also travel to see my 12 grandchildren who are spread out from California to Kentucky.

Synchronicity
by Mary Hambleton

I sigh as I slide into the hot tub. I'm here to meet up with my daughter, Ericka and granddaughter, Hunter. My daughter is right, this new club will be perfect for me as I rebuild my life, widowed after almost 25 years I am trying to find my way to a new life.

I smile at the cute guy sitting across from me; he's watching two boys jumping in and out of the pool, probably happily married I think as he smiles back. We make small talk and I'm thankful when I see my daughter and 10-month-old granddaughter appear. Small talk with cute guys while in a bikini is something I'm also getting used to, weird after so many years of married life. I've tipped my toe into the dating scene recently and it hurt, so I've taken a more cautious approach now and joined an online dating service, Cupid.com.

After swimming and playing, it's a quick dinner and bed time for my granddaughter. I head to my office down the hall, I've moved in with my daughter and son in law while I try to figure my life out. I've sold or gave away most of my belongings and feel in limbo.

My inbox blinks with a new email from one of the guys I've been "talking "to on Cuipd.com. "Oh WOW, Ericka you have got to see THIS!" I call to my daughter. There smiling on my screen is that cute guy from the hot tub … I guess his real name is Rob and he wants to exchange names and pictures... "Butterflies!"

I need to back up a bit here and explain, my profile on Cupid.com doesn't have a picture so "cute hot tub guy", aka… Rob doesn't know what I look like. I have a friend Nancy Ames, who taught "Attracting Your Perfect Mate" workshops. I helped Nancy market her workshops and I'm applying those principles to this new dating. I've made my list of all the things I want in a "Perfect Mate" and have written my online profile to include all the things I'm passionate about. I want to get to know someone on the intellectual and soul level before I put myself out there again, besides I'm a Marketing Professional who is active in our small community and I don't want my face splashed all over the internet.

I digress, for the past several weeks "cute hot tub guy" and I have been corresponding back and forth without knowing what the other person looks like or their name and now it's Show Time, YIKES!

"Well send him one", my daughter says.

Simple. So simple. Except, I'm scared. What is he isn't attracted to me? I mean we've talked. I thought he was super cute but was there attraction on his part. Yikes, here it goes… My fear of rejection is pounding in my throat as I type "I can't believe this, we just meet in the hot tub at Club Northwest tonight. I was the one in the black bikini waiting for her daughter and granddaughter. I don't have a photo that shows you more than you've already seen. Ha-ha…and I'm pretty sure those aren't legal…Ha-ha. Here's one of me at a business meeting a few weeks ago. Talk to you soon, Mary" I hit send before I can chicken out. Tasting the fear and doing it anyway.

"Synchronicity "is his reply. "PS … I like your smile. Want to work out together?"

And so, it begins short little emails and working out, disc golf with his son and finally a real date just the two of us. I'm falling fast, he's everything on my list.

Oh… My list… My "Perfect Mate" list: Loves dogs and kids, doesn't want more kids, wants a real partner not a Mom, smiles and laughs a lot, open, honest, transparent, loves water like I do, has or wants a boat, doesn't play games of the heart but likes to play board games, likes to hike and be outdoors, loves to read and wants to grow, real – not a pretty boy, loves sex, a non-smoker and a light drinker, and CUTE!

After a couple of dates, I'm starting to get scared, Rob is just what I've asked for. Have you ever noticed that just when things are starting to go the way you want them to FEAR rears its ugly head? "I'm not good at dating." I tell him. "I'm a very decisive shopper; I know what I want, what make, model, year. I know what options I want and even the preferred color BEFORE I go car shopping AND I know what I'm will to pay for it"

"So now I'm a car?"

"No, it's just well… I have a list."

Laughter, "Well I have one too".

"Really? Are you serious or are you just making fun of me?"

"Yeah", more laughter. "I will show you mine if you will show me yours."

"Seriously, you're not just making fun of me?"

"Nope! I did some work with the gals that wrote the book, "Attracting your Perfect Customers" when I was in Austin, Stacey Hall & Jan Brogniez. I put those principles to work here as well as with my company, Soul Canyon. It's all about using the *Law of Attraction* and that's what I teach, synchronicity!"

It's been over 15 years now and we've steadily built our marriage and our company Soul Canyon Training & Development on the guiding principles of authenticity and transparency. We help our clients tap into the strength that lies in the canyon of their soul where synchronicity happens.

"Synchronicity is what happens when your heart sings with your destiny and opens the doors fully to the gifts of the universe", Rob Hambleton

My advice to anyone wanting to rebuild their life for whatever reason is to get really clear about what makes you happy. Who you are. What your core values are. And then go after it with gusto and a list!

About Mary Hambleton

Soul Canyon Training & Development
www.soulcanyon.com
mary@soulcanyon.com
541-218-7601

Mary Hambleton, of Soul Canyon Training & Development shares her wisdom from a wealth of real world experiences and practical knowledge. Mary understands the importance of combining fun with learning and will always have you moving, laughing and sharing as you gain insights from her "down to earth" training style.

Mary has over 20 years of experience and success in real estate, travel, hospitality and other key industries. With a breadth of experience Mary can relate to almost any person or situation.

With dozens of specific and realistic examples to learn from, Mary's high energy presentations are engaging, fun, interactive and loaded with tips, tricks and techniques to make you more valuable.

Training topics in which Mary specializes are teambuilding, interpersonal communications, conflict and stress management, leadership and personal development.

Mary lives in beautiful Southern Oregon with her husband and business partner, Rob and their two beautiful Labradors, Bella and Sunny. Together they have 5 children and 8 beautiful grand children ranging in age from 23 to 4 months which makes family time fun, chaotic and perfect.

An Unwelcome Gift Gave Me My Strength
by Mary Knippel

Dear Younger Me,

I'm writing today to reassure you that you have a blessed life. You have always had a blessed life. And I want you to remember that you are a blessing. Please embrace this with all your heart. I know that life seems unfair and you question how you will ever achieve those secret dreams you keep hidden from the world. Know that you are cherished and loved by the God who created you. He will make it possible for you to realize those dreams because He gave them to you in the first place. So, have faith that He will sustain you through every kind of challenge. We have a phenomenal future ahead!

With All My Love,

Me

> *"The things we overcome in life really become our strengths."* Ann Bancroft

Imagine a beautiful autumn day, the air is crisp, and the leaves are turning beautiful golden shades. You walk out to the mailbox and retrieve a handful of envelopes along with a copy of the November New Yorker and O Magazine. It's around your birthday and you recognize the handwriting on a pink envelope postmarked Florida. A smile spreads across your face in anticipation of the funny card inside. One item with a familiar return address catches your eye. Immediately, you set aside everything else and open the unassuming white envelope. Unfolding the single sheet of paper, you scan the form letter to take in the information. The red X on the form letter causes your knees to buckle.

I don't have to imagine that scenario. I lived it.

I was that woman who was your average stay-at-home mom and happily volunteered at school and church. The woman who was happy to defer to my husband's wishes on just about everything in our life. I loved always being available to bake homemade pizza, sew dance and skating costumes, and drive our daughter everywhere.

Until that letter arrived…for the second time!

I received the first form letter on another crisp autumn day four years previously. I was in remission…or so I thought.

Then I opened the second letter to see another Red X in the box across from the words "Abnormal Mammogram."

How could such life-altering news be delivered in a form letter? I felt disrespected and unheard. Like I didn't matter.

With my first diagnosis of Stage 0 breast cancer, I couldn't get back into my routine and my life fast enough. I wanted to be "normal" again. My family was relieved to dive back to our way of life where my to-do list was all about them and rarely about me.

The second time that form letter arrived; my breast cancer journey resulted in the same diagnosis of Stage 0 and lumpectomy treatment. I didn't lose my hair or have any invasive procedures. I was lucky. However, others who had suffered with hair loss and more questioned whether I actually had breast cancer. I got angry. My surgeon certainly thought so or she would not have scheduled my surgeries. I thought about all the other women getting these letters and wondered how they coped to make sense of the turn their life had taken with their diagnosis.

The facts state that one in eight women will be diagnosed with breast cancer in her lifetime. How dare the world treat me like a statistic! I am not a statistic.

The second form letter arrived 12 years ago. The cancer is gone and so is the old me. I am now on a brand-new path. I made a decision to use my 30-years of experience as a journalist to share my story. I'm speaking up to help other women embrace their stories and claim their voices.

No more form letters!

No more being overlooked.

No more putting myself the bottom of the to-do list.

I make self-care and me a priority.

My voice matters! My story matters!

Your voice matters! Your story matters!

Don't wait until you have a health crisis to make yourself a priority.

If you don't like your story, you can rewrite it!

Now, you may be shaking your head in disbelief after that last bit about rewriting your story. It's true. You can rewrite it. You don't have to invest in fancy equipment or learn a new skill. I guarantee that you are very proficient at it right now!

I found a prescription at the ends of my fingertips as valuable as anything my doctor prescribed. What's this incredible tool? Journaling! I began writing in my journal as an 11-year-old. It was a critical part of my healing on my breast cancer journey and continues to be an integral part of my life. Through the pages of my journal, I have rewritten the story of me and have come to view breast cancer as a gift. A gift because it brought me clarity about what is important in my life. It brought me a confidence in myself to speak up for myself and for the women who remain silent. I am their voice until they are ready to speak for themselves.

Journaling is a beautiful way to have a conversation with yourself on the page, weigh the pros and cons of an argument, access your inner wisdom, and dream out loud and invite your imagination to express herself.

I believe that if you commit to 5-minutes a day, you will see a difference personally and professionally in your life. You will be amazed what you will discover when you take dictation from your subconscious mind, listen to your inner guidance.

Want to get started? My suggestion would be to choose the same time every day to show up on the page. Pick out a pretty notebook with a fast-writing pen. At the top of every page write the date, time, and describe where you are sitting. Set an alarm and do not look at the clock and just write until the timer goes off. Keep your hand moving to maintain the connection between your hand and your heart.

Your story matters and you are the only one who can tell it from your perspective. Your story matters and I promise you there is someone out there waiting for you to share it. And because I want to encourage you in any way I can, I've created a journal as my gift to you. I've included inspirational quotes to get your creative juices flowing. When you are inspired by you're the wisdom of your own words my wish is that you will see you have overcome whatever challenge you face with strength of your own making.

You can download it with this link.

Gift link: http://yourwritingmentor.com/meknippel2016jgift/

I'm delighted to send you this gift to unleash your creativity! It is a simple journal to download and help you develop a writing practice. I have included tips to invite your creative muse to inspire you on your writing journey. Enjoy!

About Mary Knippel:

Best-selling author Mary E. Knippel is fiercely committed to guiding you to unleash your story worth writing. Mary understands that often people feel that they don't have a story, and that it doesn't matter. Using her 30 years as a journalist along with the power of storytelling, she helps you craft your powerful message, so you feel seen and validated. And potential clients recognize that you are whom they need. A two-time breast cancer survivor she used writing and other creative tools in her recovery and chronicles the results in her upcoming book, The Secret *Artist*. Learn more at www.yourwritingmentor.com

Section 2 - Mindsets of Balance and Power

Selfish is a Thriving Mindset: by Ann Evanston

I have always been a "selfish woman". At an early age I saw the value of the "Mindset of Selfish." Taking care of myself to be better for others just made sense. Maybe it was watching my mom never really have a sense of the beautiful butterfly she really was. Having a selfish space and time for her "self" in her home was actually locked in the bedroom that she shared with her abuser. To this day I still don't think she has been able to claim her space as her own. Yes, she has her home, and is in it every day, it feels like a safe prison versus a space to nurture, grow and be creative. It isn't a cocoon that allows for transcendence.

As I started my career out of college, counseling abused and neglected teenage girls, I learned about the importance of my own "Sacred Space". My home was always this "cocoon" of sorts. It is a place to tuck away and "Be Selfish". And as my career evolved and I worked with more and more women and hearing their stories of stress, loss, frustration, and loneliness that space was very important.

But, like I share in my book, The Influence Factor, I had to Empower my Truth to truly have a space that created my cocooning and transcending (like the butterfly). See, my "real life" stopped me from creating this sacred space. Not one, but two, house fires: the destruction of space, of things with meaning all gone, led me to believe that "space" really did not matter, that things were not that important. Truly claiming my space was not important for many years of my adult life. And although I had a loving home with a wonderful husband, I, not much unlike my mother, had a safe prison, one that did not allow me to cocoon and transcend.

I knew had to change this story forever to become the woman I am meant to be in the world, I needed to have the mindset of "selfish" and create a space that was filed with beauty, energy, love, abundance. Getting in touch with the true spirit of "who" I am allowed me to create a space that was 100% all mine…inside and out.

One cocoon is my home office. It is a glorious space full of light and natural wood and inspirational quotes and color. (Feisty Red is the primary wall color if you were wondering!) This room has changed my life and business tremendously! It welcomes me every morning. It encourages my creativity. It nurtures the speaker and coach in me. And selfishly, it is all mine.

So many women take their space and its purpose for granted. There is no conscious ritual to creating it. I live with intention in my entire home now. I have taken each room that thought about the parts of me that need to be nurtured in that space. I have done little things that allow me to walk into that space and be reminded of its intention. Selfishly, I have many sacred spaces in my home now. Each one that engage my senses, awaken creativity, allow me to BEcome. As I have transcended once again and work with sexy, bold, brilliant women wanting more in life…this was necessary!

The mindset of selfish is not a bad one, contrary to our childhood lessons. Selfish allows us to nurture the parts of us that allow those we love in. Selfish allow us to be better for the world and how we are meant to show up each day. Selfish allows us to release the negative and bring strength, courage and vulnerability to every situation.

Since 1997, I have traveled the world speaking to audiences of women about stress, owning their lives, being empowered and happy. I recall once teaching a seminar in Bath England. A woman came to me at the break wanting to speak privately, tears in her eyes. She shared with me a story of how lost she is, pulled in every direction in her life. Her manager, her husband, her mother, her children all seemed to take priority in her life. She wanted to take care of herself first for a change and wanted a resource to take with her, something that could help her learn to care for who she is. That's why I am called again to bring my psychology of success and self-worth back to women once again. Today I meet women just like her. Beautiful, amazing women, with no place to selfishly call their own. Mostly because they don't claim it.

While facilitating my Champion Circle with Women this week, a woman said: "it seems so selfish Ann, and I think selfish is bad."

I find this isn't an uncommon statement from women.

The mindset of selfish is a good thing on many levels:

when you need to rest, nurture or take care of you;

to have healthy relationships, you set boundaries for yourself;

for advancing your career;

while developing connections for greater influence

So be selfish on occasion.

As you read through the stories I selected on "mindsets" you will hear women making changes in how they think to have the life they truly want. I have always said: "we must train our mind to change our life." We thrive when we let go of our self-sabotage, we think happy to be happy, and when we have been in the darkness and know how we think must change first!

(This story is adapted from one written on my blog)

More About Ann Evanston

I, Ann M. Evanston, focused on success for women. I delight in process of how we become influential, how we step into our own personal power in person, online, and in front of groups. I show women how to discover and then balance feminine and masculine energies to achieve what they desire in their lives and businesses. Strong, powerful, loving, and being uniquely you is a possibility. Because every woman has the potential. You can learn more about my passion for becoming a selfish woman as well as take my FREE assessment on the pillars of self-worth here. http://www.warrior-preneur.com/about-ann-evanston/

Playing Your Note: by Julieanne Case

After my parents divorced, my mom, my sister, and I moved in with my mom's sister and her two daughters. Mom rented our house out. I was dealing with the loss of my dad and the loss of living in our own home. Now we were sharing my aunt's home. My mom, my sister, and I shared one bedroom. There was no place to call our own. We were never told this was our home too.

In addition, my mom and my aunt competed with each other using their kids, us. The younger of my cousins, Joanne, was a year older than I. Living together, Joanne and I were constantly compared. The doctor had told my aunt that Joanne was mentally retarded. It may have been dyslexia or that she was a slow learner, but those were concepts unknown at that time.

Joanne and I would be in the next room, and we would hear things like this:

"Joanne is really beautiful, but Julie has the brains." Or *"Julie is really smart, but Joanne has the beauty."*

Joanne grew up believing she was stupid, and I grew up believing I was ugly. Yes, it took a huge toll on both of us. I remember feeling my shoulders slump. It seemed more like my whole being slumped. And no one could convince either one of us that those things weren't true. Our mothers had spoken, and they were the final authority. It was pretty much cemented in our psyches.

My mom, my sister, and I finally moved back to our house when I was

about twelve. Mom often had to work at night and I was in charge. I had to be the adult and hide my fears, especially since I was the one who begged my mother to have us move home.

One night, as my mom was getting ready to go to work, my fears were triggered. I said, *"What if I get kidnapped?"*

My mom's response was, *"Don't worry. They'll drop you at the first streetlight."*

This pretty much confirmed for me that I was truly ugly, and that meant being smart was the only asset I had.

It gave me more incentive to get an education and to get a good job so I could move out on my own. Women were always told that men didn't want smart, they wanted beautiful. A woman going to college was an anomaly. They went to get a husband, an MRS degree instead of a BA or a BS. I could give up getting a husband, I didn't want one anyway, so being smart was my way to go.

In addition, I never did anything right. I didn't even clean the house right. When things went wrong, it was somehow my fault, too. My self-confidence was pretty much non-existent. Yet, I learned how to hide my fears and appear confident.

I had begun questioning my beliefs but I hadn't come to any realization yet. I had, however, begun to change my belief concerning Joanne. My body image belief was still pretty entrenched.

JOANNE and JULIE

A few years ago, I was looking at old photographs and I was stunned by what I saw. I saw this amazingly beautiful young woman, and it was me! I realized that I had wasted so much time hating how I looked and I cried for many reasons. I ended up writing a blog post about it called, "You Are Enough Just As You Are." In realizing this, I realized there were a lot of things that I believed that may not be true.

I never believed that anything I did was good enough. I compared my art to other artists' works and mine always came up short. My writing wasn't good enough. You get the idea. The list is long!

In the last couple of years, I got introduced to Kyle Cease, and I've gone to a couple of Kyle Cease events. I really enjoy what he says. He brings a lot of unique insights and does it with humor. It really clicked with me. I watched a video where he talks about his love of harmony. When he starts singing harmony with someone, he often finds that they join him on his note and there goes the harmony. His point with this is that we have to hold our own note in our life. I felt like someone hit me between the eyes.

I've spent years comparing myself to others, comparing my more voluptuous body to the so-called perfect image, comparing my programming abilities to others, comparing my brain, comparing if I'm as loved as another is loved, or comparing my art or writing to others. Is theirs better, or is mine? I drove myself crazy. I was constantly seeking approval or validation and working to do it surreptitiously, so that no one would find out how inadequate I felt I was, or how inept or unloved I was. I also would find excuses to not paint because I was afraid that what I had done was a fluke and soon I'm going to prove that to myself, because my next one will be a major flop. So why start it?

At one of the Kyle Cease events that I attended, he delved further into the holding your note concept. It hit me full on, sitting in the audience when Kyle talked more fully about this concept. I realized at that moment that no one can paint my art like me, no one can cook like me, no one can write like me, no one can teach like me, and no one could program like I did. Only I can play my note the way it needs to be played. No one can play my note better than me. NO ONE! I was given my note or maybe notes. If I look at all the talents I have, maybe I have multiple notes to play. Or maybe, when combined, they form my own chord.

We each have our note to play, however we choose to play it. That note may be simple or complex, yet it is unique to each of us. Comparison becomes a non-issue then, doesn't it? No one can have the same note as you and you can't have the same note as anyone else. We all have a note we must learn to play and play it well. It's what makes me, me! And it makes you, you!

We are each unique. You are the only one who can truly play your note to the fullest. Play it loud, and play it with joy!

About Julieanne Case

Julieanne Case came from a left brained world, having been a computer programmer who worked on the Apollo mission that landed on the moon. Due to circumstances orchestrated by God/Universe/Source, she joined the growing ranks of the right brained world starting in 2001. She became an energy healing practitioner in 2004 and has studied various techniques. She is a Reconnective Healing Practitioner, an Intuitive Healing Artist, and a blogger. Her paintings are filled with amazing healing frequencies, light and vibrancy. She also teaches art and Drawing on The Right Side of the Brain. She assists you in rekindling the child within that leads to your creativity and your joy! We each have a Creative Soul inside. It's time to awaken it to bring about your best you!

http://julieannecase.com

Sucky Surviving Life to a Thrilling and Thriving Life

by Ondrea Lynn

Far too long the Divine Feminine has been suppressed, repressed, and falsified to be soft, weak, and unintelligent. You can look at this from a victim standpoint; feeling bad and not doing much about it or pushing your female beliefs on everyone and doing too much. My suggestion is to take a whole different approach. Choose to look at how powerful feminine energy must be for so many souls to be threatened by it which makes them push it away and never embrace it. Women who fully embody the balanced Divine Feminine reside in a place where flow exists complete with compassion and unconditional love for themselves and others. Are you ready to fully thrive in all areas of your life?

In 1995 I graduated performing arts college in NYC and began auditioning for all types of roles. During my acting career I was hired for a short time to be a stand in for Sex in the City with Sarah Jessica Parker. At this time in my life I was very insecure, and my feelings of unworthiness were palpable. I am sure that was a big reason I didn't land as many acting jobs, as they could sense my insecurity Sarah Jessica Parker was playing the role of Carrie Bradshaw and during one of the episodes she says, "*Don't forget to fall in love with yourself first.*" Back then I really didn't understand that and could not possibly even give that any consideration. My life was all about the struggle to survive then. Yuck! If you are really ready to thrive then the first and foremost important thing you must do is know and truly believe in the depths of your heart that you are beautiful and perfect just the way you are right here, right now, even as you read this. All of us are created by the same Universal energy that is Divine which makes us perfectly Divine beings.

The core relationship you have with yourself is the key to all other relationships. When you don't have a good, positive, supportive, strong connection with your own soul this will show up in other relationships. All of your relationships are mirrors to your own soul growth which means every time an "issue" arises in any of them it is an invitation to turn inward and notice where your relationship with yourself is not in alignment. I have found that when I do this and fully understand it then my relationships realign, this even includes your relationship with money. The secret sauce to this is, stand in your own truth without forcing it on anyone.

Life is full of loss, failures, and moments of starting over. My journey has had bumpy roads and times of feeling as if I was being thrown off a cliff from being a survivor of sexual assault, an unhealthy marriage, having a baby in my 20's without a career in place, and failing at my first entrepreneurial endeavor to the point that I only had $1.00 in my bank account and had to put gas in my car and feed my family. *"I am thankful for my struggle because without it I wouldn't have stumbled upon my strength,"* stated by author Alex Elle really gets you to look at life very differently. The main two principles I learned in my late teens once I began studying metaphysics that has gotten me through is; one, remain positive and two, believe in a higher power; Source/God and your higher self (your I AM presence). Combined, this will improve any situation. Remaining positive to me means there is always a silver lining, find it and keep your focus there. Believing in a higher power means co-creating with Source/God. You are never alone and when you focus on the positive Source backs you up with more positive. Knowing and feeling supported by Source brings a feeling of safety which creates a space for you to let go of any control, you think you have, and begin allowing.

Ready to move out of a sucky surviving life and into a thrilling thriving life?

Five fast track tips to follow:

1. Stand in your truth and remind yourself daily how Divinely beautiful you are
2. When "issues" arise reflect inward to understand what needs to be shifted
3. Find the silver lining in all situations to remain positive
4. Know that Source/God is supporting you and your safety
5. Remember you are a co-creator with Source for your life so the choices you make will be backed up with that energy.

Thriving does not mean work harder, longer, and force to make things happen. Thriving happens when you allow the Divine Feminine to flow, knowing you are worthy. You deserve to have everything you ever wanted in all areas of your life. Maya Angelou hit the nail on the head when she said, *"The question is not how to survive, but how to thrive with passion, compassion, humor and style."*

About Ondrea Lynn

Ondrea Lynn is a certified intuitive personal trainer, health counselor, fitness nutrition specialist, transformational coach, metaphysical counselor, ordained minister, and energy healer. She has extensive experience in multidimensional wellness. Her efforts in fitness have been featured in an article and on the cover of Woman's World Magazine. She appeared as a personal trainer on Lifetime Television's Mission Makeover, season two. Ondrea has helped hundreds of people reach their personal fitness goals, and improve their physical and nutritional health, as well as their emotional and spiritual well-being.

Check out my website and receive your free gift today. Together let's thrive! www.ondrealynn.com

Your Greatest Gifts Are Disguised
by Lisa Meisels

Have you ever wondered what why it is that some people seem to have it made in life while others struggle with so many difficulties? I have pondered that question many times over and found that our greatest gifts are offered in disguise.

I grew up wanting so badly to be "in" with the popular girls. I thought they were all pretty and everyone liked them. It wasn't only their looks that made people want to be around them though. No, it was their charisma. They loved life. And I wanted that.

I grew up feeling shy, unfortunate-looking, awkward and nearly invisible. I was always trying to get out from under my older sister's shadow. She was one of the popular girls and I was the "little sister". I felt like a nobody for most of my growing years.

All my life, I wanted to fit in, be normal and be liked. In turn, I became a perfectionist, a people-pleaser. During this time, I was very cruel with my self-talk. (I would never think of speaking to anyone else the way I mentally spoke to myself.) As I began to pay attention, I realized that I critically judged my every single thought and action. I didn't know it at the time, but this would keep me on the never-ending hamster wheel of guilt, shame and judgement.

I spent many years with an emptiness, sadness and loneliness which I stuffed. At that time, to others it seemed I had it all together. I had a successful job, marriage and 2 beautiful children. But on the inside, I was a mess. My husband at the time was never home and I was left with 2 babies in diapers, a full-time career and quite a commute. I was exhausted, overwhelmed with life and determined to be both parents at once to my children. I was constantly saying "yes" to every request and "doing" for other people. It made me feel useful, worthy and accepted which I thought were well worth the toll of exhaustion.

The twisted pattern of negating my feelings to care for others to make myself feel good continued.

Taking care of and feeling responsible for my family and those around me eventually cost me my health. I never said "no". I had no solid boundaries. I was always available for everyone. And because I didn't listen to my body for so long, it finally yelled at me forcing me to take notice of how I was living.

This happened several times where my body just said "stop". At one time all I could do was lay in bed and listen to my meditations- something I never had time to do. I didn't have time because I would stuff every spare moment with another to-do task. Another time when I was getting over a long illness, I was physically exhausted and didn't have the mental capacity to do much of anything except feel bored. I decided to get out the old paints and I started creating again. I thoroughly enjoyed it. Creating was something I hadn't done since I my children were younger because I didn't make time. I wasn't in the habit of slowing down to enjoy my life.

There were more signs of my body yelling at me to slow down. The health issues piled on. I became bored with my job and frustrated with the constant management changes. Eventually I felt a calling to do something different. But what?

I tuned in spiritually. I listened to my intuition. I took inspired action. I began to realize that as I felt more passion and joy, my body felt better. My symptoms would decrease each time I took a step toward my dreams. Each time I felt challenged and overcame my fears, I felt lighter and stronger. The more I turned inward listening to my higher self and following what felt joyful, the more fulfilled I became.

I dove into personal development. I hired mentors to help me emotionally, spiritually and in my relationship and business. I realized that when I focused on my dreams, I felt unlimited! I felt unstoppable!

Of course, as any human being, I slip back into my mental habits every now and then however as I continue to be the observer of my life, I no longer stay stuck.

What changed? I realize that my physical body is finite. There is only now. My heart has opened. I have learned to look inward for validation, nurturing and love instead of outward. The more focus I put on taking care of my needs and the more time I spent doing what feeds my soul, the better my life becomes in all areas. I've seen it with my own eyes.

Loving myself and making me a priority has been a long and hard lesson. What I now know is that this is very common among high achievers, leaders, innovators and those who strive for excellence in service to others. Having gone through this my own self, I now have a much better understanding and a more compassionate perspective for others struggling as they move through their own life lessons.

What I believe is that the challenges and hardships we encounter in life happen for us and not to us. They happen for us so that we can gain understanding and compassion for ourselves and those around us.

I believe these experiences that we see disguised as past traumas or challenges are our greatest gifts. I am now able to serve other women with the gifts I have been given which lights me up! My soul sings with fulfillment.

What have your life experiences gifted you? What can you now see are your greatest gifts and how will you use them?

About Lisa Meisels

Lisa Meisels is an Online Visibility Strategist helping women called to transform lives and make a positive impact in the world gain clarity, confidence and visibility. She helps you take a stand for what you believe and attract people who have been waiting for YOU. Lisa says your uniqueness is your brilliance.

Her personal journey and professional experience in online business, radio broadcasting and hosting the Empowered Living show and the Expert Interview Series allow her to offer her clients a powerful combination of expertise and resources that help them stand out, get noticed online and become client magnets.

Website: www.Femanna.com

Professional Survivor

by Surya Nycole

From the day I was a born, Happiness & Hope filled my house. Over the years, Pain & Confusion began to invade. They traumatized me with bullying, emotional and physical abuse, divorce, and multiple rapes. My house, was no longer safe. I tried to fight back, I tried to leave, but all I could do was freeze. Each trauma had no justice, and I began to lose trust in Happiness. They fed me lies, that there was nothing I could do, that if I would just ignore them, they would go away, and Happiness would stay. So I hoarded every tear, I wanted to cry, as Pain & Confusion slowly began to take hostage of my life. I began to lash out and smoke. I drank just to numb myself, and cope. Hope warned me, I was being destructive, but, I believed Confusion when it told me, my actions were productive. Every day I fought to survive, as Pain & Confusion tortured me, with memories, blame, and lies. They crept into my day dreams and made them nightmares. Happiness had no place to thrive, and all I could do was hold onto Hope, as I barely got the chance to say good-bye. No matter how much I would pray or lead worship at church, I was losing my self-worth. There wasn't a therapist or medication I could take, to just make them "go away". Happiness wasn't coming back and Hope, surely wasn't going to stay.

By my 30's, I was miserable. Even though I still held on to Hope, and Hope did all it could to hold on to me, I started to recognize that desire it had to leave. I began to reflect on Hope's unconditional love for me. Through Happiness's existence and distance, and through Pain & Confusion's persistence. I realized, if I lost Hope, I would lose me. So, I began to use all I had learned to get Pain & Confusion to leave. I did what many Pastors' had said, but praying and ignoring the triggers, only allowed Confusion to take over my head. I used all the tools the therapists had given to me. Even screaming "I am in control" only to have Pain & Confusion rolling and laughing on the floor. I coped using the ways of the world, but no matter where I would go or who I was with, it proved all this advice, was just a myth. Nothing life had brought, or taken from me, had prepared me. Using others advice, allow me to survive, but now I was barely holding on to my life.

Hope saw my determination and knew, I was ready to use the weapon of truth. With the final ounce of courage I had left, I attacked! I re-lived every horrific memory, going through each year of physical abuse, and faced living in everyone else's truth. I grieved every single date that I had been raped. I started to see, how someone else's Pain & Confusion had allowed them to viciously hurt me. Pain & Confusion became infuriated as I began to forgive without one apology. I grieved my divorce and began to understand, I always had the upper hand. They swarmed around me like a violent storm, so, I flooded them with every tear they had forced me to hold in. Pain & Confusion saw I was gaining strength as I used truth to dismiss every lie I had ever heard and told. They were furious! They knew the only way to conquer me was to kill Hope. So, Confusion began to use some I trusted, in my family and church, to invade me with deception, which made me question my purpose here on earth. But, Hope encouraged me that the battle was not over, but soon it would be. That truth will lift the clouds of Confusion and heal every weeping wound Pain had caused. Uplifted by Hope, and burning with truth, I began accepting responsibility for allowing Pain & Confusion to use and consume me. They fled my house, as they could now see it was not a place I would allow them to be.

While in recovery, Pain & Confusion constantly threw triggers at my door. But truth continued to prevail, allowing my deep wounds, to heal into gorgeous, unbreakable scars! Now I can see, I had been avoiding Pain by only focusing on Hope. Letting Confusion settle in, only to feed me lies, while they plotted my demise. Hope taught me in recovery that surviving with Pain & Confusion, did not make me a survivor, dealing with them did. That Pain & Confusion's presence meant I need to process. So now when Pain comes by, I focus on Hope and use my weapon of truth. I turn Pain into Purpose, and Confusion into Clarity. Pain & Confusion can no longer get in the way, and Happiness has a permanent place to stay. Purpose and Clarity have now taken over my life! I live to speak out about the unspoken and give light to the unseen, because Hope has shown me, it is critical to begin the healing.

About Surya Nycole

https://www.instagram.com/suryanycole/

Surya Nycole, is a vivacious God-fearing woman, loving special needs Ma'ma, spiritual writer and worship leader. There is never a dull moment in her life! She ministers daily from personal experience by walking with men and women around the world through their pain with her transparent, yet witty, encouragement and guidance. Her thought provoking style, boldly speaks out for those whose voice has been silenced and inspires those screaming to get theirs back.

Live a Life You Love
by Erica Hoese

I've been around fitness most of my life-- my dad was a wrestling coach for 14 years, my brothers wrestled, and I was active with swimming and volleyball. I grew up around the weight room and we always had some sort of protein powder in our pantry. It wasn't until college that I became a little more obsessed with being thin and making sure I didn't gain the dreaded "Freshman 15." I did what most do, I thought sweat and salads were the way to lose weight... and I did, but what I didn't know was most of the weight I was losing was muscle, not fat.

Fast-forward a few years later— I got married to my wonderful husband, had 2 amazing children, and I found myself partnering with a nutrition company as a health coach. I chose this company because of the products, their reputation, and their advancements in the wellness industry. I also felt very confident that my children would be able to use these products safely too. In the first year, I gained 16 pounds of lean muscle. I learned that results come from 80% of your nutrition, 20% of your exercise, and 100% of your mindset.

In the fall of 2013, I went on a business retreat which happened to be one of my most pivotal moments in my life. I was unhappy with myself and the amount of success that I thought I should have had by now. My husband and I were thinking about adding to our family and I was feeling very pressured, which was put there by me, to figure out how to run a successful business and be a mom.

During this retreat, one of our group activities was to break a board. Out of 20 or so people, I was one of 2 people that couldn't do it. In reality, breaking a board has nothing to do with your strength. Your technique, sure, but it has <u>everything</u> to do with what goes on inside your head! My thoughts about myself were beating me up inside and it felt like I was drowning, trying to come up for air. During the weekend, I had a breakdown and an amazing talk with two of my mentors, one conversation about what I defined as success, which turns out I was actually doing pretty good.

The second, about having another child. I had all these limiting beliefs about how I couldn't run a successful business with 3 kids. She said, "Don't think of what it <u>can't</u> do, think what it <u>will</u> do." I want to live life without regrets, so my husband and I decided to have another child.

After I got home, I was feeling pretty good and confident about everything. Then I logged onto Facebook and that's when I first saw my picture-- someone had taken it at that exact moment I was having my breakdown, unknown by me. I was mortified! I felt humiliated that other people would see this. What would they think? Now everyone would know the "truth" about me.

In November 2013, I became pregnant with our son. Because I'm a "type A" personality and kind of a control freak sometimes, we had planned this pregnancy around a business trip that usually takes place in October. I found out I was due in July, 3 months before, so it was all working out perfectly.

Well, a few weeks after, it was announced my business trip was moved to one week after my due date. I was so angry. I started feeling resentful, discouraged, and that's when all my negative thoughts came back full-force. I became depressed, I was unhappy with myself, I was jealous, I was comparing, and I was looking everywhere outside myself for validation.

It was during this pregnancy that I had my biggest breakthrough.

I realized three things:

1. The only person that could change my life was me.
2. No event in my life could take the place of who I was or define my worth.

3. Everything I do is my choice.

I made a decision in January 2014 to get back in the gym and become stronger, both physically and mentally. I had Jace in July of 2014 and in August, I started eating healthier again and doing things for myself, instead of for other people.

The gateway to the mind is through nutrition and fitness. Our life is based on moment to moment choices that will lead and shape us. Every day we get the choice to begin again. I believe having a powerful morning routine can set you up for massive success in your life. I can speak from experience that my life was more chaotic when I didn't put myself first. How you start each day is going to determine how you show up. **You** get to decide.

About Erica Hoese

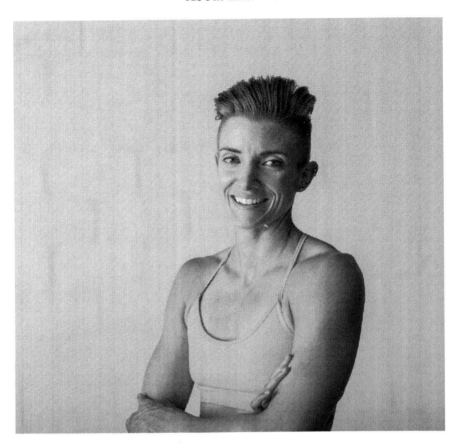

Erica Hoese is a wife, mother of 3, fitness & wellness coach, natural figure competitor, and speaker based out of Minnesota. Her passion is teaching moms how to reconnect with who they are, embracing strong— not skinny, eating healthier, and loving themselves from the inside out, so they can be happier, healthier, and better moms.

She's been helping moms for the past 5 years with their health & fitness-- helping them redefine success on their terms and living a life they truly love. She believes you can have the body you desire, that you can meal prep and make healthy meals that your whole family enjoys, and that you truly can have it all...

whatever that means to you. She believes it's a combination of having support, resources, pace, & passion.

That's why she's created the #FitMomArmy: a tribe of women who lift each other up in all aspects of life.

When you put yourself first, it allows you to show up in a bigger way, which results in deeper relationships, inner peace, and a more fulfilled life. It isn't just about your appearance, it's about being healthy from the inside out and working on all aspects: mind, body, & spirit.

Please reach out any time,

Erica   Hoese
erica@xo-erica.com
facebook.com/erica.hoese
instagram.com/erica.hoese

Free gift

"If you'd like my exact morning routine I teach my clients, head to my website: www.xo-erica.com and sign up-- it's my free gift to you. Thank you for reading my story and allowing me to share something that is very close to my heart."

Turns out I look good in pink!
by Debbra Lupien

Who are the five most important people in your life?...

Got your list ready? Let's review. Now, tell me are you on the list?

When I first saw this message, in the form of a meme, it hit me right between the eyes. It had never occurred to me to put myself on that list, let alone in the number one position. But that's exactly where you, and I, should be — first on our own list.

What do they tell you on an airplane? Put the oxygen mask on yourself first or you can't help anyone because you'll be dead!

I have this vivid memory: It's my sixth-grade self, off to school one day wearing a favorite pink dress. I felt so good. I **loved** that dress! But when I entered the classroom, a girl walked up to me and said: "There's something about you and pink."

I wanted to fall through the floor. I didn't know what it **was** about me and pink, but surely it was a bad thing. I never wore that dress again.

A few years later in high school I was talking with a friend, lamenting that I'd probably **never** get a boyfriend because I had no personality — she agreed with me! I really needed better friends.

This was my truth for far too many years. I didn't speak up much because I thought no one would be interested in what I had to say. Mostly I was invisible. It took a great many years before I began to understand my value and take off the invisibility cloak.

That's what **my** massive inferiority complex looked like and those memories are a painful reminder. Can you relate? If someone looks at you in a peculiar way does your mind automatically jump to a negative conclusion about what they're thinking?

Contrast my experience with my daughter's: At the age of four we were driving when she said to me: "Look Mommy, that man waved at me. I'll bet he thinks I'm cute." I treasure that memory of my little girl secure in the knowledge of who she was.

The thing is, we don't usually know what the other person is thinking. We get to decide. What if we always decided it was something good? That's how it should be, confidence in who you are and your value. Not interpreting every sideways glance as a negative thought. In truth that person may not even be thinking about you at all.

A Giant Step Forward

In my thirties I was inspired to start a business. It wasn't easy, but I was driven to control my own destiny, so I persevered, ultimately settling into creating custom databases. I was good at what I did, and my clients appreciated help with organizing and simplifying their business. But inferiority hadn't yet been rooted out.

When I at last achieved that sought-after pinnacle of six figures, I felt like a fraud, a pretender, like I didn't deserve to be there. You see, I was one of only 20 companies chosen to work in a "partnership" relationship, getting the best referrals from the software company we were all certified under. How could someone like me, self-taught, be as good as these geniuses with their programming backgrounds?

I grew more and more uncomfortable with the situation ultimately self-sabotaging and letting it all go. My business had outgrown my vision of myself. That wounded girl still lived deep inside me. No matter how far I had come, or what I had achieved, she remained.

Finding Myself

Fast forward to the present where I have reinvented myself as an Akashic Records Expert. It took a number of years to come to this place, but it's where I was always headed. It's my soul purpose and now that I have healed that wounded girl, I help others find their soul purpose and heal their own wounded child.

It didn't happen overnight, it was a process. As I worked with the guides of the Akashic Records they kept reinforcing the message that *you are not broken, there's nothing wrong with you.* In fact, in their estimation *you are a magnificent, brilliant, resplendent soul.* Sure, you have battle scars but that's life. Where you are right now is perfect, and tomorrow you will be more perfect. It's a journey. Stop torturing yourself over perceived flaws!

Over and over this message came for clients and by extension me. When the truth and love of the message finally penetrated those layers of self-recrimination and loathing, I had a massive transformation.

Do you remember in the movie *The Secret* when Bob Proctor kissed his hand and said, "I love myself?" At the time I saw that it was incongruent to me that anyone could feel that way. Now after spending time helping others, and being helped, I can honestly say I **do** love myself. Where I am is perfect. It's the result of the choices I've made and tomorrow it will be more perfect—just like you.

Today I share this story in presentations with audiences of multi generations. So many women are undervaluing themselves—it's practically an epidemic. I urge you to put yourself first. Nurture yourself. Allow for the possibility that you **are** amazing and perfect just as you are right now in this moment, and tomorrow you'll be more perfect. There is not another like you in the Universe. You **are** special. When you finally embody that truth, then you'll be ready to change the world.

Guess what else I learned? I look great in pink!

About Debbra Lupien

Website: AkashaUnleashed.com

Debbra Lupien is the Author of *Akasha Unleashed: The Missing Manual to You*, and an internationally recognized Akashic Records Expert. She specializes in helping women discover their soul purpose, embrace their magnificence, and unleash their potential. Debbra believes The Akashic Records are your birthright. A powerful tool intended to be used to help you create a magnificent, even magical life. When you need answers, when you want to understand yourself better, when you're ready to discover buried treasure, consult your Akashic Records. There the truth will be revealed: the treasure is you and it was all along.

Well-Being Attunement Meditation

This guided visualization is especially calibrated to help you reach wellbeing and remain there longer. Relaxing and refreshing with incredible visuals. When the stress of the world becomes too much, when you need an energy reset, use this meditation. It's like taking a mini vacation. http://akashaunleashed.com/akasha-unleashed-well-being-attunement/

It Was Never About Outside Insecure
by Carole Cueroni

Being in the flow of life, high in your vibrational energies and consciousness, living from your heart center is such a beautiful, awakening experience. It is when you come to realize that you have within huge personal power to access the life you desire and want to co create with God, the Universe, your higher power. It is never too late to make the choice to change your inner consciousness and dialogue living the life you have always dreamed from your heart.

It's the ego, the subconscious, the fear in our minds, fear from people in our lives that we give our power over to. This truly creates a life of unhealthy choices, trauma and more diseases we create for ourselves in life's journey. We allow past lives and personal past experiences to interfere with our daily lives giving them our voice. Change is hard. Many a time there are circumstances we don't even understand, get stuck in, but choose not to change because change is very hard. The fear becomes part of our daily energy leaving our self-esteem, self-worth and self-love as the biggest lost pieces.

It was after a sexual assault I found myself caught up in unhealthy relationships and an abusive, controlling, narcissistic relationship in marriage. This life event caused an internal paradigm of undeserved love, kindness, respect and caring for myself. It was my inner dialogue. This paradigm affected my love for myself, acceptance for myself, the way I viewed relationships, sex, my self-confidence and my inner personal power.

I was able to keep these emotions separate from my successful professional career. My professional career was outside solid and inside my heart was locked up in undeserving love and judgement. I needed to forgive myself first for what happened, then others, to let go of what wasn't mine to own.

Relationships were not relationships from an open loving heart. I was closed to feeling love. I felt empty inside. It was a co-dependent relationship of unworthiness inside and a fear of not being accepted by the outer world. If I found myself getting close in a relationship I created self-sabotage that drove them away or I just bolted. I made choices in men that were not available emotionally.

How I felt about myself directly affected my relationship choices. During my marriage, I allowed the manipulation and control purely because of my feeling of unworthiness. I allowed childhood learned behaviors my mother modeled from her own traumas, fears and an unhappy marriage to play into my life. I felt unworthy inside of love.

It wasn't till my father passed in January 2002 did it hit me that I could not live in this life any longer. With my father gone I could see more clearly the abuser I was married to and how it was affecting me and my children. It took every bit of courage and strength to create a plan to get him out of our lives. Many friendships had stopped coming around because they feared him. My support was faith in God, the Angels and the Universe knowing I had the strength to do this. I got him out of the house and filed for divorced. Everything material was lost. I knew I had a huge challenge in front of me with three daughters to raise and support.

The lesson to learn here was never about being outside insecure. It was *inside insecure* and how to change this in my inner self. I had my personal power in my outer world, professionally and how I presented myself to the world. It was my inner world that was rocked, wounded and totally unworthy of receiving and giving love. I had to make the decision to fix what was broken inside me to be able to life the abundant, beautiful life I imagined.

I started learning more about conscious awareness and heart centered healing teaching myself how to get out of old paradigms, learning to trust in my intuition, God, the Universe, my higher power. I learned I could co create the exact life I desired without limiting beliefs and through living from my heart. Today I stand confident, proud and in love with myself in the most beautiful way owning my total personal power. I am living from my heart. I learned how to live from love now not fear and judgement. Lessons become wisdom. This is now what I coach and teach.

I love who I am now. I am confident, successful and happy. I co create my life each day. I truly live from my heart every day with love and compassion. I am open to receiving and giving love at its purest. Ready for the love relationship I desire and deserve. Nonjudgement, forgiveness, gratitude and meditation are daily practices. The lesson in this for me was I had the power to change my circumstances all along through changing my negative thoughts, removing my fears, living from my heart center of love, forgiveness of myself and others to make this fore filling change. I trusted to become my authentic self, taking back my inner personal power. Life is filled with intuition and synchronicity, miracles and magic every day. You just need to be in awareness to see them, receive them. If you trust in your institution, your guides, your heart you will find the true

North Star within you to follow. We can only live in this present moment in gratitude and appreciation for all we have. Yet, set our desires in intention for infinite possibilities and live truly feeling as if the life you co created in your heart is your present reality. Watch for the signs as your dreams become your reality. It is a truly beautiful experience.

You place your dreams in a beautiful golden place in your heart. Then co create dreams and live feeling them from your heart as they become your present reality. They will show up in divine timing. Trust in yourself and the Devine guidance. Decide to take the leap of faith. The life you co create is worth it. There is a little bit of magic in everything....

About Carole Cueroni

Carol Cueroni is an entrepreneur and life coach specializing in Living your life story through the joy of conscious awakening through your heart, energy healing and angle work. She is a second level Reiki practitioner and light worker. A few of her mentor coaches have been the Tony Robbins institute, Dr. Dave Kruger, Mentor Path, Jeannie Spiro, Angels with Doreen Virtue, Collette Barron Reid, Oracle Training. Dr. Alison J. Kay, PhD Energy Healing.

Carol's had a profound Angel saving of her life in 1992. Her connection and invited participation in 1988 with Dr. Herbert Benson, Harvard, in The Mind/Body Medicine program was the beginning of her journey for going inward, learning to use her mind to heal and aligning with her soul, purpose and living her joy. Carol has also done business startup and product placement consulting since 2007 with her consulting business. In 2011, she was a product panel speaker on the kick off tour in LA of Tory Johnson's, Spark and Hustle small business tour. She has had a long successful retail career with Federated Department stores, Boston in senior management positons in finance and distribution during her twenties. She was the Vice President of Distribution for Record Town, Albany, NY at 30. She owned martial arts studios for 20 years.

She is currently working on her own book, I Danced with Angles which is about her life's journey of experiences being saved by Angels and her greater purpose here on earth. She is also working on opening a healing and arts center near her hometown in Massachusetts. Carol is the mother of three daughters. She is passionate about making a difference in the lives of others every day. She loves family traditions, cooking, music, dance and traveling to learn about other cultures. Carol can be reached at carole@livingyourlifestory.com. Her website is livingyourlifestory.com. Also at carole@theblisspointe.com. And her upcoming website theblisspointe.com.

.

The Day I Arrived
by Ally Loprete

Since I was a little girl, I had dreamed of being a television talk show host and having a platform to bring positive insight that would transform the world.

Now here I was.

I should have been relishing in the moment, but instead I found myself paralyzed and terrified. Before I could make sense of what was happening, I felt my entire body go numb. Frantically trying to make sense of what might have triggered this unexpected condition, I began to spiral into the abyss of worry.

My paralysis threatened to demolish my life-long dream. *Why was this happening... NOW???*

As I spiraled down, familiar thoughts of self-sabotage began to flood my mind. I couldn't shake the notion that I was about to experience the downfall of my career, the moment that I'd forever refer to as the time I sat in complete greatness before I completely lost it all. I saw myself opening my mouth to speak only to begin sobbing uncontrollably, humiliating myself in front of the entire production crew and permanently branding myself as the girl who had a melt down and a complete loss of her emotions. Down - down - down I spiraled.

This is it, I thought. This is as close to the finish line as I am going to get. I'm about to sabotage the moment I've been waiting for my entire life.

As these thoughts percolated, I felt my throat chakra lock. Any minute the show runner was going to call me to the stage and I wouldn't be able to speak. I couldn't fuck this up. I couldn't lose this moment.

I tried to search for a new thought that would distract me and pull my focus away from the destructiveness I was creating, but I couldn't seem to find one that was more resonant than the thoughts that were causing me to decline. It felt impossible to do on my own, so I quickly texted Anna Mae, my "life-line" soul-sister who just gets me. She is the kind of friend who speaks my language, has the ability to see clearly when I've become blinded, and knows exactly how to get me to shift my perspective on command.

> I am on the set. Having a panic attack. Any minute producer is going to call me to the stage. Tears are starting. Can't speak. Help me shift my focus with a new thought. Please get me out of this!!

> Oh, Ally.
>
> This is nothing. It's just an old pattern.

That was all I needed.

Of course!

This wasn't a punishment, it was a gift! Suddenly I knew that this horrifying moment I'd experienced many times in my past was showing up again —as an opportunity. This was my chance to shift! Once I surrendered myself to its message, I could see I had a clear path to advance beyond this pattern once and for all.

Instead of looking back at this moment from somewhere in my future, imagining it as the time I destroyed my career, I consciously imagined myself remembering this experience as one of the greatest positive shifts in my life. Somewhere in my future, I was already sharing this story to the world.

I had already begun re-writing my narrative! I felt a sudden physical transformation come over my entire body. My throat tension released. The welling of tears in my eyes threatening to ruin my makeup had suddenly dried. It felt effortless.

In that instant, I remembered who I was as a professional talk show host and interviewer. Ready and in the zone, my insecurities vanished, I called upon the essence of what I do best. Stepping outside of my limited interpretation, I gave my full attention to the guest I was about to interview... and that's when I saw it!... My guest was in the process of having an anxiety attack!

Tears were filling her eyes, she was gasping for breath, and I knew that she needed my help. I never would've been able to see it had I not cleared up my own vibration!

As a seasoned radio broadcaster for several years now, I knew that my job as a host was more than just looking and sounding good. I was exceptional because I knew how to create a safe and invigorating space for my guests to shine their brightest. I knew this set me apart as talk show host, and likely what landed me this job in the first place. My guests loved being interviewed by me because I always made it a priority to give them the most memorable experience of reaching their highest potential.

I had to save this poor girl.

I took control even before we were called to the stage. I announced that I needed a few minutes alone with my guest, then asked her to take a walk with me. I told her that she was in a safe space, hugged her, and let her "ugly cry" as much as she could. After her release, I met her gaze, fixed her makeup and asked that she trust that I wouldn't abandon her. I made sure that she knew I understood her and that I had her back. In no time, we were ready for her interview.

What happened next was magic. Our sparkling energy was in sync and we hammered that segment home in just one take. The entire production crew must have felt the dynamic shift in vibration because just after the director yelled "Cut!" I heard the sound of applause. The director audibly howled with satisfaction for our performance.

"You," he said, "are good." Hugging me, he added, "That was amazing. You have absolutely arrived, young lady."

Suddenly I wanted to celebrate. What a revelation! Who knew we were capable of doing this? I had just consciously experienced two completely contrasting perspectives... on completely opposite sides of the emotional spectrum...and the shift was instantaneous! I had experienced firsthand the vastness of what can be achieved with just a little shift in perception.

Just like I'd promised my future self, I began telling this story right away...and I am sharing it with you now. I will forever remember it as the moment I arrived.

Just like me, YOU are completely capable of purging yourself of limiting beliefs. When they arrive, they are easy to recognize because they pose as your biggest road blocks. It's so very easy for us to default into feeling like a victim, and very difficult to believe that we have any other choice in how we react. However, when you begin to trust that it is no accident when experiences show up when they do, with practice and patience, you can retrain your mind into seeing a whole new perspective.

These are the moments that shape and define you. They are gifts that are strategically placed in your path because of the significance of what the experience will mean to you. Some deep part of your core source has asked for guidance, so when you attract an undesirable pattern into your life, what you are really doing is attracting the *opportunity* to find a solution. In other words, the object that you most desire will show up looking like the polar opposite of what you were hoping for. However, there is another side to the coin. Once you learn to move through it to the other side, you will reach the object of your desire. This means that every one of your undesirable patterns are actually gifts. All it requires is some receptiveness and a sense of adventure.

About Ally Loprete

Self-made momprenuer, Ally Loprete is nationally recognized as a public speaker, radio personality and television host. She founded OurMilkMoney.com, a nationwide online business directory of self-employed parents, and hosts iHeart Radio's THIS LITTLE PARENT STAYED HOME and DRAMATIC IMPACT WITH ALLY where 6 million listeners tune in for resources and support. Ally is one of the co-hosts on WAKE UP, a nationally televised broadcast for the new mainstream. Her book *You Got This!* is now available on Amazon. In addition to inspiring a movement of entrepreneurial parents, Ally is dedicated to advancing women's leadership worldwide. http://www.allyloprete.com

Section 3- Expectations and Balance

Knowing Your Expectations: by Ann Evanston

I met a guy. Like a REAL guy. Like life partner GUY.

Let me back up. It was a wet, rainy, winter evening in Seattle, and my roommate Mary and I were getting dressed for a night out. In our twenties, and single, what else would we do on a Saturday night? We had our favorite place, Sharky's, lovingly nicknamed "the shark tank", but we always went there. Tonight, we planned to check out a new spot that opened.

We left the townhouse early, wanting to be able to get a table and not wait in line outside in the February chill. Yes, this was the OLD days when you just got a table because it was available, not because you paid for a bottle to get one, lol! As we drove around looking for parking, we started to notice the, ehem, "clientele" of this new bar. They were looking a wee bit sketchy, and definitely not dressed up!

Mary looked at me and said: "Annie, no way! Let's go to Sharky's."

So off we went. It was extremely early, parking lot empty and the DJ was not playing yet, but I knew the bartender Mark very well. We stood with him at the bar ordered drinks, laughed and talked.

Suddenly, my body tingled with energy. This sensation made me turn towards a far entrance. It was like radar: beep, beep, beepbeep, beepbeepbeepbeep, beepbeepbeepbeepbeepbeep!

I zeroed in on this tall, gorgeous man. As he walked around the corner where I could no longer see him, I turned to Mary and Mark and said: "I will have that man before the night is over."

They both laughed as they knew me well. I was the "love them and leave them, fuck 'em and forget 'em" type. I wasn't looking for a relationship, just fun!

I ALWAYS got my man.

I made eye contact while passing closely by the DJ booth. He asked me to dance. We danced and talked the night away. It was almost like we came there together. Mary even caught a ride home. I was enjoying this man, not bored at all. Besides being REALLY cute and damn sexy, he was funny, and smart. We spoke about careers and dreams. He was impressed by my work with women. He asked for my phone and email, email was new and cool back then. Something in me said: "this man is so much more than a one-night stand Ann."

"LAST CALL!!!" (Where did the night go…we just got started!)

"LAST DANCE OF THE NIGHT!!" ('Don't leave! Don't leave me girl, please stay with me tonight!' Oh geez, this song really…he's TOO sexy!)

LIGHTS UP! (He's still beautiful with the lights up!)

"Ann," he said, "My friends are all going to Minne's for pancakes, why don't you come with me?"

"No."

Expectations. I said no because I knew where breakfast led. (At least in my view of the world!) I didn't know at that point that he went to an all-boys Catholic High and was an altar boy! But that didn't matter, I knew myself. And I didn't want to screw this guy (which I easily could have). I wanted to know him. I wanted him to know me.

Expectations are a cornerstone of self-love. They create balance and personal power. We thrive with healthy expectations of self and others. We must first know what we expect of ourselves and others before we can communicate it. Within each of these stories you will hear how women have had to clarify their own expectations with emotions, sex (yes of course!), and ultimately with themselves.

Oh, and that gorgeous man? Well, he is the love of my life. Earl and I have been together ever since!

About Ann and the Earl

I, Ann M. Evanston, have been married 20 years, yes to the same man. Earl and I work hard to have a relationship other people DESIRE to have. My grandmother taught me that deep, true, loyal love does not come without trial and tribulations. Commitment and great love takes work. It's easier to walk away. We plan to start our own relationship podcast called "Love Porn" because you cannot hide in great relationships! We "grow food, not lawns". We have a 9000 square foot, high density, organic, year-round garden in our ENTIRE yard. I post pictures all the time on my Facebook profile where you are welcome to follow me, my adventures with Earl and our passions!

From Resentment to Empowerment
by Isabel Hundt

My husband and I got married in 2010. We knew we always wanted to have children, but we wanted to wait at least 2 years. I had just moved from Germany to the US and when we decided to get married we only knew each other for about a year.

In fall of 2012 we decided that we wanted to try getting pregnant without worrying too much when it will happen. After two heart-wrenching miscarriages we found ourselves pregnant with a healthy baby boy. The pregnancy was heavenly from the beginning to the end. I had never any morning sickness, he slept whenever I did. He was awake whenever I was. I felt so connected to him that we had our own conversation about expectations and life. My very personal gift is not only being highly highly sensitive toward the energy of others, but also seeing colors around everything but especially people which always has a specific meaning. Sometimes the color is connected to the struggles someone is going through and what they may want to consider moving forward and other times it is rather prophetic.

For my little boy I always saw the color gold. The color of triumph, success, prosperity and especially wisdom. He sure is an old soul. I enjoyed the experience of feeling so close to him, to have visions about his life but more importantly he let me work on my business. I had enough energy throughout this whole pregnancy to move to new levels of success. Jonah was born December 20th, 2013.

We couldn't wait to take him home. I was certain that I could continue with everything I was up to businesswise as before. I hadn't even considered anything else. Well, as you may know, having a newborn is a whole different world. I was so sleep deprived at times that I couldn't think straight. The first month went ok. It is easy to drop work over the holidays. But I knew I had to get back into it starting January. My business didn't run on its own nor did I make any money just dreaming about the success as an entrepreneur.

With each day I became more irritated, frustrated, overwhelmed and angry. I started to have one mastitis after another. For those who have gone through it know that it feels worse than having the flu….or at least about the same. Jonah started to be colicky and I just wanted to hand him over to someone else. Don't get me wrong, I wanted him, I loved him, but I started to feel resentment toward him. I wasn't able to combine the dreams I consistently had about my work and mission with being a mom. My heart was burning for more. There was no room anymore for the work my Soul yearned for so badly. I also didn't have any family or friends close by to help me out. So, whenever he did sleep I worked no matter how tired I was. I could feel my temper creeping up slowly over time. I wanted to scream. While I went through the struggle of identity crisis his colic became worse.

In my desperation I called my own coach and cried and put it all on the table. That is when everything changed, my aha-moment which created a profound shift within myself, my business and my life in general. Finally, one day my coach called me out on my stories and beliefs. Together we worked through all the dirty stuff that brought up even more emotional baggage from years ago, including the miscarriages. I had to realize that my emotional state impacts my son's emotional and physical well-being. Once I was able to let go of the resentment and anger I felt, within 24 hours he was colic-free.

I started to see the science behind what emotions are, the impact they have on myself and those around me. I saw that if I am emotionally not prepared and emotionally not ready to receive the dreams and the goals that I had set out for myself, I will never get there physically either. I will continue to sabotage my own success and my calling through ridiculous head talk and beliefs and stay emotionally imprisoned.

Emotions bring color to our lives. As briefly mentioned, I personally have the gift of vision and to see colors around people, therefore to me emotions are a beautiful and stunning dance of colors of different vibrations. Our experiences of life are unique. We create our own reality by the way we choose to see and acknowledge whatever is going on inside of us.

Emotions really are powerful and instead of running the rat race, we can create an empowering symphony of colors of different vibrations.

If we are honest, most of the time we have no idea what is really going on inside of us. We feel, and we feel a lot. We are being told how we should or shouldn't feel. Media is trying to tell us which emotional state is best for us to be successful in life. Everything just becomes this huge ball of knotted yarn of emotions we can't seem to untangle.

Can you imagine what would be possible if we can really use our emotions as a guide instead of seeing them as a hindrance no matter what we experience? How much more confident would we feel? How much more driven, ambitious and empowered?

It doesn't mean that we won't have any negative feelings anymore or won't feel down at times or wish our children would just magically disappear, but we will be much quicker in creating awareness and are able to stop the spiral down before it manifests into something we'd regret.

Your emotions are something to listen to. Everything has its purpose. And the closer we listen, letting go of trapped emotions, the more guided we will feel, and the more understanding we will have of our journey in life.

About Isabel Hundt

Isabel Hundt is a Speaker, Life Transformation Coach, Author of The Power of Faith-Driven Success, Empath-Warrior™ and Emotions Clearing Practitioner.

She supports Empath-Warriors™ (highly sensitive people) and EmpathPreneurs to conquer the world, experience deep felt freedom and peace by understanding the energy around being an Empath, teaching tools to protect themselves emotionally and energetically and by setting the foundation to feel guided from within, to understand their life's purpose and calling, to have a bigger impact, improve performance and to reach their goals faster.

Isabel also teaches how to use our emotions and intuition as a powerful guide in business and life.

Website: www.isabelhundt.com

Free Gift:

If you get influenced easily by everything that is happening around you, you want to grab your free guide "5 Simple Ways to Protect Yourself from Negativity". This guide shows five simple ways to protect yourself energetically and emotionally from toxin-overload and overstimulation of the nervous system. You will find exercises you can implement right away.

Link: www.isabelhundt.com

Heart Thoughts
by Karyn Leigh

After nearly 14-years in a "traditional" marriage, I left to respond to a long-time call to open relationship. It was the hardest decision I've ever made because I have two sons who continued living with their father. I didn't have other partners at the time, but my heart had known for years that I needed the freedom to love more than one.

Two years after separating, I met the man who feels like my mirror half, David Francisco Ortega. We both used the term ethical non-monogamy in our OK Cupid profiles. It's as if we are the masculine and feminine version of each other on a soul level.

The first months of our relationship we spent mostly in my bed, pillow talking and ravishing each other for hours on end. By month four, to each of our great surprise, we decided to look for a place to rent together. Shortly thereafter, despite our highly unconventional financial profile, we landed a magical home with a huge backyard we call Tranquility Base.

As any soul contract does, this romance turned committed domestic partnership has evoked deep shadow only now ready to step forth to be integrated into d'light.

David is energized by engaging with his loves. We joke that he is neither introvert or extrovert, but a *sextrovert*. He has cultivated the ability to attend to each of his sweeties and be a fully committed domestic and romantic partner to me.

I always feel a bit "zingy" when I know David is having a sexy date with another love but have felt the most stretched when he starts to date someone new.

The initial months of our domestic partnership brought up some huge unexpected challenges for us to grow through.

We had just come back into rapport after I'd violated one of our agreements. We'd been "just housemates," and even gone to a couple's therapy session before he could share a bed with me again.

He and I had barely reconnected and he was all excited about a new relationship. I couldn't conjure joy. All I felt was grrrrREALLY????

In the thick of an emotional upheaval one morning while David was pleasuring me orally—not usually what takes me over my full orgasmic wave— I had what I can only call a heart thought arise of its own volition.

I was caught up in mental gymnastics over if I could handle staying in partnership with David. I thought I might be too sensitive, that despite our transparent communication, his sincere adoration and full commitment to our foundling household, that his way of being open was too great a stretch for me.

So, imagine my surprise when as David loved on me unaware that I was spinning in doubtland, a thought arose of his latest sweetie feeling like the most beautiful woman in the world. I suddenly wanted her to have pleasure as never before during their date that night. As these heart thoughts arose I began to enjoy a symphony of sumptuous sensations unparalleled by anything previous. I returned to my body receiving the most delicious yum ever. Heart thoughts continued to flow forth wishing this immense pleasure and total wellbeing for each of David's other lovers as his kisses took me over one of the most luscious orgasmic waves ever.

During our pillow talk afterwards I marveled over what had transpired. David beamed a smile brighter than ever as I described the surprise. I received confirmation to continue with our open partnership and learned that blessing his other loves during our intimate sweetness increases the good for all!

How illuminating to discover that my heart thinks! I've since come—pun intended—to trust my body's responses to what I call my pleasure oracle for all kinds of key guidance.

What do I attribute this to and how might others be benefitted by their own heart thoughts arising? I have a practice of surrendering everything to the divine, the one pulsing heart of all life, Love, Grace—call it what you will. I offer the breadth of my imagination from ecstatic visions of peace, prosperity, and pleasure for all, to dark snark, pettiness, and terror. By allowing the full spectrum of thoughts to express, I don't bypass the healing humor in acknowledging I have as many ungrounded fears and insecurities as anyone. Even if the terrifying "what ifs" never come true, it's important to give them voice.

Heart thoughts showed me that not only can I relinquish all my worries, doubts and judgments, but that in doing so my heart will intervene when I need it most. True heart thoughts are confirmed by my pleasure oracle then root and blossom within my physical body.

My physical temple will not allow me to stay in a relationship configuration that is not serving me and the whole of creation of which I am part. I can trust that whatever evokes pleasure is a confirmation of yes. When pleasure is evasive it is an invitation to slow down, listen and communicate with my heart and other's hearts in even more explicit, direct ways until we reach mutually good yeses, or can honor ourselves and each other with a no thank you.

Through a recent experience with yet another new woman who was not a good fit from the outset, I've learned to ask David to include me before he becomes lovers with a new woman so that each of our hearts may speak openly and freely before there is sexual exchange in the mix.

The best counsel I can give for you to discover your own personal oracle of pleasure is to cultivate a direct relationship with your heart. Place one hand on your heart and one on your belly and breathe deeply. Speak or write directly to your heart. Pour everything out and request its loving guidance. Ask your heart to communicate yeses through your turn on and orgasm.

Each woman's journey is unique and certainly all will not choose to share a beloved. No matter where you find yourself in the relationship spectrum, may your heart guide you to bliss, connection and peace beyond your wildest imaginings.

About Karyn Leigh

With self-love & laughter as companions, Karyn lives, breathes, writes, mentors and speaks about ethical non-monogamy, sacred sex, and heart-centered living.

In the Fall of 2017 she founded the Human Connection Engineers in the San Francisco Bay Area to reconnect humans via stealth operations to encourage more human to human interaction in public. Karyn had a fantastic time getting her B.A. from UC Berkeley and is dedicated to lifelong study of psychology, physiology, sexuality, spirituality, and human potential. After 11 years in Europe, she returned to California and worked for her alma mater as an integral part of a small team that raised more than $6M for graduate fellowships.

When she's not exploring sexual ecstasy or writing about it, Karyn's probably mentoring a client, tending her temple home and fruit trees, taking a long walk in nature, cycling with David, or watching one of her two sons play soccer.

FREE GIFT

Karyn's currently at work on her first full length book <u>The Yoga Of Open Relationship</u>. The first 11 women to send an email to KarynLeigh0011@gmail.com with subject: Heart Thought Conversation, will receive a complimentary 30-minute "Connect With Your Pleasure Oracle" phone consultation. All others will receive advance notice of Karyn's book release and an $11 credit toward the book purchase or any other product/service offered.

Get Happy First!
by Dr. Jennifer Rozenhart

It all comes down to believing in your worth. Every decision, every change, every movement in life comes down to if you believe you are worth more. Many of us are fortunate enough to have great self-worth instilled from our upbringing, and many are not. While this is a critical piece of self-worth, it doesn't mean that you still won't have challenges along the way. I was blessed to have two wonderful parents who consistently demonstrated that I was worthy, of love, support, prosperity and joy. To this day they are married 50 years and I always look at them in awe of what they have created together. All I ever wanted was what they had, yet I had no idea how to get it. Even with that very positive experience in my home, that did not prevent me from making some decisions where I did not honor myself.

Growing up, I had experimented with alcohol, drugs, and making poor decisions with men. What did not sway was my desire to be "successful" - I continually made good grades and graduated at 25 years old with a Doctor of Chiropractic degree, with academic honors and clinical excellence. I married and had my wonderful son at 32. I was under the false pretense that because I appeared successful academically that everything would turn out perfectly. I wish I would have spent as much time in personal development as I had in professional development. I spent 15 years making poor decisions in my personal life, tolerating abusive behavior, using alcohol to escape that pain. I would be one person at my practice and be another at home.

I figured out in my late thirties that this lack of congruency and authenticity was killing me. I was putting on a mask around most people and struggling to truly find what made me happy. I read a quote around that time that struck a chord:

"Most people think it's success that leads to happiness, when in fact it's happiness that leads to success."

It was far more difficult to take off the mask than I had realized, because I couldn't just remove it. I had to become ME 100% of the time, because I deserved it. That didn't mean showing up how I was living at home at my office but changing my home life and patterns that weren't supportive of who I really was. I had to develop, evolve, into the person that my patients thought I was. I had to get happy FIRST. I deserved it. I was worth it.

Get happy first, that meant making some serious changes in my home life. First, I had to get very CLEAR headed. That meant no more escaping with wine, truly looking at my situation with a clear head and clear heart. I was going to be a divorced single mom at 40, I was going to be doing it all on my own. (Truth be told, I WAS doing it all on my own which I why I was so unhappy!) Coming to the decision was the hardest part of the journey because once I realized my truth and spoke it, there was no going back. How could I? I knew I was unhappy and I knew I would never be as successful as I had planned. To do nothing and continue to ignore my heart and spirit was not a long-term strategy I could live with. It wasn't easy, but it was so worth it.

Learning to only do what made me happy, learning who supported me fully, learning to let go of ideas, stories and untruths- this journey leads me to develop in ways that I never thought possible. I was always afraid to be seen, because I knew I was hiding some secrets. Since this transformation, I have gotten re-married to the man of my dreams and enjoying the relationship that I always longed for. Professionally, opportunities have come along to speak at National conferences, develop, coach and train other doctors with a new business opportunity. Had I not done the work to GET HAPPY, none of this would be possible. The lesson for me and that I hope you take away is that the movement towards happiness drives everything else. If you don't want to do something, don't do it. If you don't like how you feel being with someone, a friend, a partner, make a change to that relationship. It's not always easy, but it's always worth it!

About Dr. Jennifer Rozenhart

Dr. Jennifer Rozenhart, DC was born and raised in Canada and moved to San Jose in 1994 to receive her Chiropractic degree from Palmer College of Chiropractic-West. She has been in private practice since 1997 and her practice has received the Best In Silicon Valley Award from the San Jose Mercury News for 5 years.

She is an active member of Business Women Of Silicon Valley and loves to help mentor other women business owners. When she's not in the office she can be found with her family, at one of her son's games or driving somewhere fun with her husband. Dr. Jennifer loves to cook (and eat) great food and enjoys staying active.

For Better or Worse
by Connie Boucher

Some girls dream about getting married for years and plan their wedding well in advance. But that's not how my oldest granddaughter did it.

So, this is what (I'll call her Shaniqua—because it's my husband's name for every girl he doesn't know the name of) Shaniqua texted me on Thursday, the first day of a three-day convention we were attending. She said, "Grandma, (little Johnny—that's Craig's generic name for boys) and I are going to the courthouse to get married today and we want you to have a reception for us in your backyard". Now this might seem shocking to some grandmas but given Shaniqua's history and impulsive personality it didn't surprise me much.

I knew there was no stopping her, so I responded, "Why don't you wait and get married in my yard, so your family can be there?" To that Shaniqua texted back, "Who will marry us?" and "How soon can we do it?"

Back and forth we went, hammering out the possibilities (with me whispering what was going on to Craig) until it was decided that due to the late fall weather and our tight schedule the only day that would work for us was the following Friday.

That's when the wedding theatrics started.

Over the next three days of the convention I texted enough people to get the ball rolling. And let my family know what was going on. And of course, they all had plenty to say about it.

On Sunday an out of state acquaintance (invited by Craig) showed up expecting to spend the night and be entertained the next day. She was confused when I explained that we couldn't play because we had to pull a wedding together by Friday. She was NOT happy about it and to my annoyance complained until she left on Tuesday morning.

Craig, who has an exceptionally kind and inviting heart had invited another casual friend to stay with us for the next five days, so just three hours after the first one departed, Fidelia showed up. When she walked in I sarcastically smiled and said, "Hi, you're welcome to stay with us but here's the deal. We're having a wedding here on Friday so I'm going to be busy and it's going to be crazy and you're on your own". To that, Fidelia smiled and said, "Great, what do you want me to do? I'm the queen of piecework (meaning I'm pretty good at anything you can throw at me)".

Then she actually jumped in and helped nonstop until the wedding was over, which elevated her greatly in my eyes, and it's how she came to be fondly thought of as family.

But I digress. Back to the wedding which was now less than three days away. After we went food shopping Fidelia offered to take on role of caterer. This freed me up to decorate and take care of last minute stuff. Which there was plenty of. The night before the wedding our bishop fell through so Craig googled preachers and after a brief chat, he sealed a deal online.

On Friday Fidelia did kitchen duties while Craig set up tables and chairs, and I finished decorating the yard. We were pretty much ready to go by the time Shaniqua showed up, but when her aunt Julie saw her she promptly let her know her "look" was unacceptable and ordered her into the bathroom to wash her face so they could redo her hair and makeup. Of course, this attracted the other aunts who all piped in and offered advice. Once Shaniqua got past a few tears she went along with them and when they were done she agreed she looked better. When Johnny saw her, he said she'd never looked so pretty.

With Shaniqua fixed up to everyone's satisfaction the group moved outside and settled into their chairs. The preacher hadn't shown up yet, so we listened to music on an amped up iPhone while Craig called to see where he was. Finally, the preacher arrived with a large black binder and mic in hand and we started the ceremony. My elderly father walked the bride down a rock path with rose petal tossing flower girls following behind, because we'd neglected to instruct the girls to go first.

Then the near toothless preacher opened his big binder and started reading (lisping) from a giant print, sheet protector enclosed script, into a mic that didn't work, and we had no idea what he said. When he was done Johnny kissed Shaniqua and we took pictures while Fidelia brought out the food. Then everyone including the preacher dished up their plates and switched to party mode and we all had a great time!

To wrap this story up, in spite of the fact that it was a last-minute shoe string wedding with more than a couple of guffaw moments, it turned out beautiful and Shaniqua and Johnny were pleased. Most important, they felt loved and supported.

There have been many times in my life when things have not gone as expected and I was faced with a choice to either cry and resist or go along with it. I've learned that rolling with unexpected turns, rather than fighting them, makes everything a whole lot easier!

So, the next time you find yourself in a "you've got to be kidding... how am I going to do this moment", here's a plan for getting you through it. Let go of your expectations and switch to plan B fast (you'll likely need to create it on the fly), then jump in wholeheartedly and give it your best shot and laugh at all the things that will inevitably go wrong along the way!!

This, my friend, is what keeps the un-predictableness and craziness of life from tasting bitter and makes life fun and sweet instead!

About Connie Boucher

Connie Boucher (pronounced like touché) is an author and keynote speaker, as well as a massage therapist, wife, mom, and grandma to 10 kids, 18 grandkids (+1 great). Because she has a lot going on she's always looking for super simple and effective ways to get things done, hence her business is Super Simple Wellness. Connie has lived a lot of life and spent the past two decades working in the field of healing. She's passionate about helping people understand how their body-mind-spirit (physical and energetic self) works, and what they need to do to release negative emotion and keep all parts of themselves well-functioning. She enthusiastically shares her stories, insights and ever-expanding knowledge with audiences, and has fondly been dubbed "the emotional midwife" because she's so masterful at helping people clear limiting beliefs and experience true transformation. Through her "transformational" chakra workshops, speaking events, and books, she teaches "makes sense" truths and empowers others to live healthier, happier, and more prosperous and rewarding lives.

Connie Boucher is the founder of Super Simple Wellness and Transformational Chakra Experience workshops, and the author of Play dōTERRA and Pay For Your Habit, Wellness Made Simple, and Chakra Wellness Made Simple. www.connieboucher.com

Let Go To Grow
by Mary Von Ohlen

I sat quietly, listening to people share about the usual– life, love, spirituality– and many spoke of moms. It was Mother's Day 2008. I couldn't muster a share during the 12-step group that morning; but as we stood up to close the meeting in prayer, I found myself weeping.

When my friends saw my tears, no explanation was necessary. It was the first Mother's Day after losing my mom unexpectedly a few days before Christmas.

Does losing a parent force you to grow up? With seven years of accumulated sobriety, I thought I'd done some serious growing up already. I didn't know another significant life change awaited me later that year.

After some hugs from my supportive fellowship, I headed home to meet my girlfriend. In the midst of planting some beautiful potted flowers to honor my mom, I heard my phone ringing from just inside the deck. I retrieved it, assuming some friend or relative was reaching out given the difficult day.

It was from my boss. He was texting me on the first Mother's Day after my mom's death. He picked this day to send me an impulsive work request. I should've quit right then. His text was merely a symptom of a pattern of dysfunction that had been building for some time.

It was one of those moments of clarity, yet I lacked the courage to carry out the necessary action at that point. There is the type of letting go that is forced upon us– like with sudden death of a loved one– and there's the kind that requires a conscious decision, courage, and trust. It was time to take that leap of faith in my work situation.

Sometime around that period, my sponsor suggested I tell my boss I need to take a leave of absence.

Tell him you're going to take the summer off. I mean, losing your mother is the most significant loss of your life after all!

Didn't she get it? That was not an option. This man was a type A workaholic who when his own mother passed, was back in the office the following day. I may as well have sooner quit than suggest taking a month off.

By August, I realized resigning was exactly what I needed to do. I knew despite being debilitated by grief, I was far too healthy to remain in what had become a toxic work environment.

We were in the midst of a global financial crisis, so it was not a practical time to jump ship from a reliable job. Educating people on matters of health and holistic solutions is part of my life's purpose and my position allowed me to fulfill part of it. The main problem was that I was in a support role; I was supposed to be a leader rather than a leader's "right hand". I had learned all I could from my current job and it was time to break free.

My boss was on his journey and I on mine; our paths crossed for a reason, but that period had come to completion. The job and working relationship were no longer in alignment with who I was and where I was destined to go. With much personal preparation, I respectfully gave my notice the day after Labor Day.

That conscious act of letting go changed everything. I began my transition toward full professional autonomy and would never again work for someone else. In all my future collaborations, I would be more mindful to choose mutually beneficial situations with conscientious colleagues in my field.

Taking that leap of faith afforded me the time and space to move forward on my career path, as well as tend to my own personal healing from grief. In the years that followed, I would study more holistic modalities, develop additional skills, and deepen my intuition and confidence as a holistic practitioner running my own healing practice. I gained the spiritual sense to trust that if I follow my purpose and passion, I will somehow have everything I need.

This experience in knowing when to leave a situation which no longer serves me has proven invaluable more than once. I recently applied this lesson again in my professional life. I decided to let go of a collaborative project that, however enjoyable, seemed to be keeping me from the next step in my professional growth.

It was easier this time – not only to recognize the familiar pattern sooner but to act accordingly with greater ease. Based on my previous success in letting go, I was confident that positive results would inevitably follow. Sure enough, shortly after surrendering that endeavor, a wonderful new opportunity manifested in perfect alignment with the direction I was seeking.

When we can acknowledge that a situation is no longer in alignment with who we are and where we are meant to go, we can release it guilt-free to create space for whatever better thing is on its way to us.

About Mary Von Ohlen

Mary Von Ohlen is a leader, teacher, and healer. She inspires, educates, and connects people to holistic resources for healing and personal growth. Mary draws on her vast knowledge and experience across the fields of psychology, counseling, addiction recovery, physical health and wellness, energy healing, spirituality, alternative medicine, and more. The common thread among her endeavors is her passionate dedication to empowering others to continually expand their awareness and realize their own authentic power. MaryVonOhlen.com

Be Kind to Yourself, Always

by Sarah Neiswonger

One of the best pieces of advice I have ever gotten came from my therapist, who I saw for several months after an ugly divorce. I was there for anxiety and depression, rooted in trauma from the relationship. In sessions, I was timid and fidgeted obsessively. Expressing my feelings brought me to tears most times.

I had spent a lot of time walking on eggshells with a person who would blowup at the drop of a hat with explosive anger, and I never knew what would set him off. I remember one incident in particular that always seems to come to mind when I think about this. I was on the phone with my credit card company and needed his card, which was linked to the account. I asked him if he had it on him and, without checking, he said no. I then asked if he could check, just to be sure, since I had the rep on the line already. Big mistake. The exchange turned into a huge unnecessary fight. I could go on for days with stories just like this.

In the end, I opted to just try and stay silent in order to avoid fights or took the blame when I was hurt by the words or actions of others. This left me feeling like I could never express myself or my needs, and that I was constantly waiting for some unknown disaster. At work, I had trouble asserting myself, and I began to feel like nothing I did was quality work, even tasks I'd done many times before. As I explained these feelings to my therapist, she said:

"You need to be more kind to yourself."

So simple. My internal dialogue had been warped and I needed to consider how the negativity was affecting my quality of life. All of these obsessive and anxious thoughts were simply unkind to me, and I had to put an end to them. When we think about being kind, we tend to think about kindness to others. We rarely think about being kind to ourselves. When you take time to think about it, it's interesting how being kind to yourself comes in so many forms. It can be taking care of yourself physically or unwinding mentally. But, it can also take the form of asserting yourself or not taking someone's particular brand of bullshit. You get to decide what's kind to you.

I used this principle as a guide and applied it in many ways. I had been working on my health and fitness and decided that being kind to myself meant making sure my health came first. This meant that, as much as was possible, I would schedule life around my diet and exercise, making it a priority. Not only did I surpass my goals, I inspired others. That's the thing about treating yourself well — when you do it, others around you treat themselves better too.

I applied being kind to myself at work. I stopped judging myself so harshly and forgave myself more readily for small mistakes. I gave myself pats on the back for a job well done. I gave myself breaks and took time out of my day to clear my head.

Three other very important applications in the workplace were to assert myself more and having confidence, and to stop comparing myself to others. These are not common ways to show kindness, but the principle applies. Knowing what you deserve, knowing your own worth, and making sure you are treated accordingly are major kindnesses. I was no longer afraid to have these tough conversations or, rather, I had the conversations anyway, despite being scared, because I was being kind to myself first and foremost. Many of us avoid conversations we need to have because we lack confidence, are afraid of the consequences, or feel we're undeserving of a change. Don't let yourself fall into these traps.

When it came to comparing myself to others, I was doing it every day, and I was making myself miserable with obsessive thoughts. I was competing internally with my peers even though, realistically, I knew there was no need. Contrary to being kind, this line of thought is very cruel. You never actually know how well anyone else is doing, so it's pointless to compare yourself. Even if they look like they're on top of the world, they may be struggling, and you'd never know. You should compete only with yourself; challenge yourself to be the best version of you and do what makes you happiest.

It's easy to talk about being kind to myself in hindsight. But you should know — it's not. It takes practice and quite a few failures. I thought for a while that I wasn't deserving of kindness. I had to practice and train my brain to think in that way and ask the question *Is this kind to me?* I had to catch myself in my negative, obsessive, or anxious states and actively change how I talked to myself. Whenever the thoughts *I'm not good enough* or *I'm messing up* or *I'm not attractive* or *No one loves me* crop up — and, trust me, they still will every now and again — I have to stop myself, breathe, and tell myself the exact opposite. I also look for other causes; maybe I'm overworked or tired. At those times, I need to give myself permission to take a break and do something nice for myself, and to actively acknowledge that I need and deserve the rest. This mindfulness has especially helped change my habits.

So, if you're not doing it already, be kind to yourself! Take the time to identify what kindness means to you and apply it whenever you can. Never miss an opportunity to be kind to yourself.

About Sarah Neiswonger

Sarah has found professional success in managing payment fraud detection for a large tech company after earning a degree in Criminal Justice. She's been in tech and leadership the majority of her career and is passionate about teaching and collaborating with up-and-coming leaders in her field. In her spare time, Sarah enjoys a good book or puzzle, spending time with her many pets, being a nerd, and weight lifting.

When Quiet is NOT a Good Thing
by Dianne E. Campbell

I walked into Barnes and Noble and was pulled by an unknown force to the Self-Help section. Directly facing me was an entire wall promoting a book titled, "The Verbally Abusive Relationship" by Patricia Evans. My first thought, "Oh, ya, sure. If *only* we were even yelling at each other!" But I was drawn to this book. Upon picking it up and opening it to look at the chapter titles, I was totally blown away. In a good situation you might say I had an AHA moment. It was an awakening, that was for sure.

I understood verbal abuse to be cussing, swearing and name calling. This book introduced me to other forms, including SILENT Verbal Abuse. To discover I wasn't imagining the absurd situation I was living in, to understand I was not going insane AND the most important part? To learn I WAS NOT ALONE was euphoric! Like an addict, I sat and devouring every word. This woman was writing about MY life – chapter and verse!

The most frustrating part of Silent Verbal Abuse is that nobody else sees it. I learned that this is a typical tactic an abuser uses – that the brunt of their abuse is reserved for usually one person.

To the outside world he was engaging, funny and a one-of-a-kind guy who had his act together. He came across as a great dad to both his sons and our foster-adoptive daughter. People saw him as a good husband and provider, one whose concerns were always in the right place. But this was NOT him in our private world. Once we crossed the threshold to our home and closed that door he was a much different man. Communication was non-existent and what little did take place wasn't good. Silent and moody, I believed he was in a state of deep depression. He spent his evenings in the basement, just sitting and staring at a nail. Other times he spent hours outside staring at the fire pit, justifying it by saying he was keeping an eye on the meat in the roaster. He was not focused on our future and was not providing for our present.

They say the eyes are the windows to our souls. His were empty. They were flat and that scared me. I worried about him. I loved him! I wanted the man I married back! More frustrating was when our foster-adoptive daughter was around. He immediately became that "outside person", but only engaged with her. I was invisible! I remember her trying to involve me in the planning of a future activity (she was 6 years old). Their conversation was fun. Joking and, laughing, but as soon as she included me in? BAM! He shut me out immediately, all the while making it seem to her that I was not interested. SO masterful that I honestly did not know how to respond, except to retreat and wonder did that really just happen?!

I learned these abusers are also often sociopathic and narcissistic. Certainly, they are passive aggressive and are masterful at all of it. I honestly thought I was going insane and that is exactly where he wanted me to be.

Another time he did not speak to me for 28 days. Not a word. On the 29th day, I was in the kitchen reading. He was cooking, reached into the spice cabinet, turned, looked at me and asked, "Do you know where the red pepper is?"

I looked up, the voice in my head screaming, "ARE YOU FUCKING KIDDING ME?" But, knowing that using ANY kind of escalated voice or showing any emotion only got me knocked down further, I simply said, "You have not spoken a single word to me in 4 weeks and you now ask, "Do you know where the Red Pepper is???" He looked back at me with a puzzled, condescending look and replied, "Ya, do you have a problem with that?"

I did know we were in deep trouble as a couple, but I thought it could be fixed or saved. I did not understand that his emotional state and his alcoholism had stolen the person he was when I met him OR that maybe, MAYBE, he was finally being and showing his real self, which today I know the latter to be the reality.

I look back and know I really did know that truth. There was no more "we". His emotional/ mental issues were not going away. But, I loved him, wanted his love for me back *and* we were adopting our foster child. I stayed much longer than I should have.

A year later, we could finally adopt her. A month after learning this, he walked out. He left me $25, all the bills, a child to adopt, 2 dogs and a cat to feed and he never spoke another word to me again. I soon learned he had refinanced our home, forging my signature to get fast cash. In order to adopt Angela, I had to be divorced. I got it done in 6 months and never looked back.

What happened from then to now is still incomprehensible to me. Much more took place over the next few years, none of it positive. Today, I am on a better, positive path and finding my voice with the hope it helps others.

If anyone reading this sees her life unfolding in this way, please reach out and learn about Silent Verbal Abuse– at the very least get the book. The author has since created a community of awareness and there is a big focus on the still much unknown SILENT VERBAL ABUSIVE Relationship. And, if this really is you, please know, YOU are not going crazy - It is NOT you!

About Dianne E. Campbell

Dianne has lived big business success, foster parented and met her prince who turned out to be not. In losing it all, she found her real self. Her gift is diving into YOUR being, cutting through the muck to clarify soul versus ego's desire for your personal inner peace.

She can be contacted at TalkWithDianne@gmail.com.

From Broken to Broken-Open:
How to Get Everything You Want Fast

by Jackie Simmons

There have been many books written on the topic of Broken-Open and I will not comment on them here other than to say that they are all correct. Everything you want is on the other side of Broken-Open.

This is my story of breaking-open and an invitation for you to consider making this year, the year that you move from broken to broken-open.

Broken.

I knew I was broken, damaged beyond repair. Don't get too close, I don't want you to see my brokenness. I know you feel broken too. That's OK. You are just fine the way you are. I'm not. If you could see how damaged I am you would walk away. I know you would, others have.

I lived most of my life absolutely certain that if you knew me - if you really knew me - you would walk away.

This certainty of my brokenness led me to hide. For most of my adult life I hid behind my studies and my knowledge and my busy-ness. I avoided conversations that would reveal my flawed self, my damaged core. I avoided forming relationships with those who might have helped me see myself as whole. I kept them at arms-length, I let them teach me, but I wouldn't let them mentor me because if they got close enough to mentor me, they would leave me. I knew they would, others had.

The problem is that I also avoided mentoring others. I could teach skills and tactics, I could download my knowledge in structured teaching points and tell entertaining stories about concepts and clients, but not about me. I kept my journey a secret, certain that if you knew who I was, you wouldn't want to work with me.

From a life perspective, this belief in my brokenness was a challenge that led to two broken marriages. From a business perspective, this belief in my brokenness kept me just above flat-broke.

Don't get me wrong, I worked hard, I networked my assets off. I gave talks and shared my knowledge and hid my heart. I could reach out and show you your value, until you got too close and then I would push you away.

As my protective shell got thicker, the bank account got thinner; and as my bank account got thinner, my self-confidence got shakier; and as my self-confidence got shakier, I hid more. I hid in training programs and certification courses, certain that one of them would break me free from my self-doubt.

I was wrong. One course it didn't do it, but the combination of teachers, courses, and programs; plus, the weight of over-scheduled days; added to the confusion of conflicting voices as I continued to add course upon program, finally brought me to the brink of quitting.

Before the brink, was the growing awareness that I was creating more confusion for myself with the over-consumption of other people's ideas. A growing awareness that I was sabotaging my learning with busy-ness. Then hiding from the uncomfortable awareness of self-sabotage by numbing out with food and a bottle of wine.

Finally, I could hide no more, my "brink" arrived.

I stood on the brink of quitting. Certain that the thousands of dollars I'd spent on certifications, trainings, and programs; the years I'd spent studying; and the hours I spent away from my family; were all wasted, I wasn't ever going to be anything more significant than a cog in a wheel . . .

and I cried.

In the tears, in the complete surrender, something in me broke open. In that moment of openness came the thought: "there's nothing wrong, there's never been anything wrong" and on the heels of that wondering came another thought: "nothing I had ever done was wasted." Could it be true? - in that one moment of questioning, I went from broken to broken-open.

Broken-Open: revealing what lay hidden - a Truth about life:

"I CAN'T LIVE MY LIFE WRONG"

Broken-Open Living means:

No money that I have ever spent was wasted

No time that I have ever spent was lost

No thing that I have ever studied was useless

No person that I have ever met was evil

Broken-Open Living Truth 1:
Every penny I have ever spent was well-spent, even if I wouldn't spend it that way now.

Broken-Open Living Truth 2:
Every second I have lived was well-lived, even if this second is the last second I have to live.

Broken-Open Living Truth 3:
Every word I've ever read, every word a teacher ever said, was useful, even if I can't see how to apply it in my life just yet.

Broken-Open Living Truth 4:
Every person I have ever known enriched my life in some way, even if I choose not to be around them today.

Broken-Open Living means permanent freedom from the self-critical, harshly judgmental shell around my heart.

Imagine your life, Broken-Open and free.

Broken-Open Living begins the moment you are grateful for all of your life. Grateful for all of it. All the places, people, and events that wounded you and left you hurt and confused. Hard to imagine until you make one decision.

The moment of gratitude occurs when you DECIDE that the damage inflicted upon you by the places, people, and events of your life was nothing against you. It was simply and elegantly preparing you for your path. Gratitude occurs the moment you decide to see the places, people, and events of your life as simply your fastest path to breaking free from the shell around your heart.

Broken-Open Living: Joyfully revealing what lays hidden – your uniqueness.

Broken-Open Living: Confidently exposing the contents of you heart – unconditional love.

Broken-Open Living: It's waiting for you – what if you decided that you were ready today?

About Jackie Simmons

"Breaking Open" skyrocketed Jackie Simmons' business From Secret to Success in 7 Months. BUT it didn't start out that way.

The inner saboteur of brokenness sat on her phone like an elephant in the room, stopping her from making sales calls, and distracting her so she couldn't focus and finish projects.

It was through learning to permanently tame her inner saboteurs that the Total Success Mindset System was born. Jackie used the system to help herself, and then her clients go from overwhelmed to over-the-top.

Her book: *Your Path From Secret To Success,* is a guide so that no one else's journey has to take 30 years.

Create your own success journey: start each morning with reading The Four Truths of Broken-Open Living above. You can print a copy of them below. And for a free guide to creating your personal Success Journey Roadmap go to: www.SuccessIsAGame.com

Section 4 - Finding Success

Success Isn't What I was Told: by Ann Evanston

I grew up believing that success is about what we do, not who we are. Neither of my parents went to college. I feel like I was told at LEAST once a day: "you WILL go to college Annie." I absolutely grew up trusting that. Interestingly I was also told that I would be a doctor. And I grew up believing that too.

I chose a top liberal arts college in Washington state where I grew up. With a top ranked pre-med program, recruiters told me if I got through it I would write my ticket to any med school in the country. I got in! My mom was so proud, she always knew I'd be a successful doctor.

Being a liberal arts college, I was required to take credits in ALL fields of study, not just my major. My sophomore year was rocking my world. I was taking chemistry and HATING EVERY MINUTE of class. Across campus I am taking a sociology class....and loving it! I loved what I was learning about human behavior. And by spring break, I had to declare my major.

With thoughtful consideration, I went to the administrator's office and filed my major and minor.

That year, mom decided to drive the 275 miles to campus to pick me up for spring break and bring me home. She hadn't done THAT before, I always had to hitch a ride with friends or take the bus! She said it would be great mother/daughter time driving back.

We made an adventure of it: stopping at outlet malls, grabbing a bite to eat. It was a long, full day and I did not bring up declaring my major, and oddly enough she hadn't either.

It was dark by the time we got back to the greater Puget Sound region. Mom is driving her little sportscar, me in the passenger seat. After a long day on our adventure, I think we were both a bit tired, we hadn't spoken in a while. Suddenly, mom breaks the silence. Maybe she had been thinking it all this time. She asks: "Annie, didn't you have to declare your major?"

"Yep." (Closed ended question, so I answered accordingly....I guess somehow I knew this wasn't going to go well.)

"So, what did you declare, biology? You always liked biology in high school."

"Nope."

"Pre-med then?"

"Nope."

"Annie, you went for the hardest of them all chemistry? I'm so proud of you!!"

"Nope."

"Wait, well, what's left?"

"I declared sociology mom, I don't want to be a doctor."

The silence hurt my ears in this car moving at 65mph. Just deadening. And then she said: "You will never make any money."

That was a pivotal story in my life, believing that I had to earn money to prove my success. And I can earn trust me, but it isn't success for me. I had to let go of other perceptions of my success. I had to define it for myself. The fear I felt stepping away from my family's path for my success was overwhelming, I did it anyway. It took great courage to start my own business and keep hustling when the economy sank. I now know that I am a healer, just a different kind. I heal women by teaching them self-love, the highest expression of self-esteem. I heal what stops them from being influential, powerful and loving.

And the ultimate success? It is the long-time relationships I have had with clients that stretch over decades because they love what I do and want to be a part of the adventure. Success is having a powerfully loving relationship. Success is the fun and laughter I have in my life. It is having these relationships because I am willing to be vulnerable and open my heart. That is success.

Success is tied in with fear, courage and vulnerability, as you will feel reading these amazing stories.

A Little More About Ann

Ann M. Evanston has created and turned concepts into successful start-ups for years. In college, she decided to design, develop, brand and successfully implement her own sorority (which is still running on campus 20+ years later, called Zeta Pi), to creating a non-profit organization for homeless pregnant and/or parenting teens, which is now nationally modeled.

Ann went to graduate school with the intention of starting her own speaking and coaching business. She successfully started her company in 1998 and developed an international presence as a speaker to large corporations. She has been a speaker a really long time starting toastmasters in the 7th grade! Ann competed in oratory in high school and has spoken in front of audiences as large as 10,000, and given talks paid professionally since 1995. Get my 5-step system to selling successfully on the stage here: http://www.warrior-preneur.com/bad-assery-business-toolbox-membership-program/ and have my success today!

The Many Faces of Success
by Carmen Lindner

Twenty years ago, if you would have told me that one day I would be living back in Oklahoma, homeschooling my three kids and working a successful network marketing business I would have asked, "Well where did I go wrong?". LOL! My picture of a successful woman has definitely changed over the years.

I started my career in corporate America when I moved to NYC after college and started working for ABC Network. It was an amazing experience, living in working in NYC is like nothing else out there and I am so grateful for that opportunity. I enjoyed handling accounts, building relationships & sales but started looking for another opportunity after we moved to CA. Like many people I decided advertising sales wasn't meant for me; I couldn't imagine spending my life there and was longing for something with more of a purpose other than just a paycheck. Although that paycheck was pretty fantastic at the time! After eight years, I decided to give entrepreneurship a go and started a coaching business for professional women. I loved helping women reach their goals and the freedom of being on my own, but within a year a dessert idea took off and I knew I had to run with that opportunity.

I started Gotta Have S'more in 2010 after spending some time in my kitchen and creating a unique dessert idea, which became known as "The S'muffin. It was the right time and the right place for a dessert company to take off and it was a whirlwind from the very first day. Five years later, after growing the company and making accomplishments like getting into Williams-Sonoma, and being on Shark Tank, we decided to sell the business. My husband and I had wanted to move our family back to OK, so our girls could grow up close to family and enjoy a slower pace of life. I was planning to take advantage of the low cost of living and not work or start anything else besides homeschooling my kids and being a mom, but that didn't last very long.

I still had a passion for business, marketing, branding, health and coaching. My friend, Tami, knew I would love being a representative for Plexus long before I knew it myself. Throughout my life I had always said that I would never work a network marketing business. My perception was that network marketing companies were scams, the women involved were working 24 hours a day, not really making a true income and having to bug people all the time. That might have been true in the 90's but the industry has come a long way, many of the companies have changed their structure to benefit the representative, with the help of social media there is unlimited marketing, branding and networking opportunities and if you get with the right company the income is very real and consistent.

Today I spend most of my days at home or running the kids around and their education is my number one priority. I'm able to get my business fix, work with my friends and make an income from my phone in between school lessons and soccer games. It's a far cry from a corner office in NYC but I wouldn't change it for the world.

I've learned so much along the way and am grateful for every opportunity because I'm able to use every skill that I've learned in the corporate world and as an entrepreneur to benefit my home-based business now.

The lessons I've learned are, don't let fears stop you from making changes, or taking advantage of an opportunity. Keep an open mind about career changes & don't be afraid to jump into something even though you don't have any experience. Don't let other people's opinions stop you from doing what you know is best for your family. Networking and meeting new people will never be a waste of time.

About Carmen Lindner

Carmen Lindner grew up in Oklahoma. After graduating in 2000 has worked in advertising sales in NYC and CA, after eight years she left the industry and started her own Professional Women's Coaching business, Successfully You, where she enjoyed helping with their own business and personal goals. In 2010 a dessert company formed right in her CA apartment called Gotta Have S'more. She grew this company for five years gaining accounts like Williams-Sonoma & making an appearance on the ABC hit show Shark Tank. After selling the company five years later and then moving her family back to Oklahoma, she started working for a network marketing company called Plexus Worldwide. With that she is currently building her own team and enjoying helping people with their health goals.

Free Gift

I always send out samples and I'm happy to send a care package, with samples, to anyone who is interested in joining our group of fun, successful, smart women who make an incredible income working from their phone by helping people improve their health on a daily basis. Ambassador ID number 1149595, contact me at

Carmenalindner@gmail.com or 917-868-1340

Be Sure to Eat Your Ice Cream
by Deborah Lopez

My mother had an expression – "Eat your ice cream while it's on your plate." She was always doing that – making the most out of her life, finding new opportunities with every challenge she faced. I realize now that she taught me how to do that by her example. She never let anything keep her down and she was able to change her life many times to get to her next plate of ice cream.

I thought I would always live in my mother's shadow. Elsie was larger than life in my hometown of Akron, Ohio. Went back to get a B.A. and M.A. after having 4 kids. On the City Council, a political leader/activist on civil and women's rights, a big Democratic supporting Adlai Stevenson, Hubert Humphrey and JFK. She played bridge, threw wonderful parties where she cooked everything, wrote campaign songs to show tunes, was an artist. I left home at 17 and moved to California at 19 to be able to make my own life far away from her universe.

And make my life I did. I broke all my mother's rules. I ate what I wanted (she always had me on a diet), dropped out of college and was a hippie, became a 60s radical at Berkeley – far to the left of my parents. I married a man they didn't think was right for me and had 2 kids in 5 years. Well, how chagrined was I to figure out that mom was right about my marriage and other things? That was very hard to admit, but it helped me a lot.

When I left my husband, I was making $6,000 a year as a preschool teacher. How much ice cream was I going to be able to eat on that? So, I did what my mom had done when faced with challenging family economics - I went back to school – law school. I got my real estate license to support us. My mom was facing political battles over abortion rights and it was time for a change for her as well. Lucky for me, she figured out that her next plate of ice cream was in San Francisco with her grandchildren. She and my Dad moved out to help me while I worked as a Realtor and went to Hastings Law School. I could not have done it without them.

My career took twists and turns that in hindsight look a lot like my mom's battles. I was in executive positions with the City and then with a private corporation that put me at odds with powerful men with fragile egos. This was the 80s and early 90s and as a woman in very high management positions, showing a lot of leadership and being successful on many fronts, I rubbed those male egos the wrong way.

145

The second time, it was a time of crisis for me. Mom had been diagnosed with breast cancer and was dying at the age of 72. That was a shock to all of us because we thought she would far outlive my Dad who had Parkinson's disease. Mom was as young and vibrant as any woman half her age. She was my Dad's primary caretaker, taking classes at SF State for a second Master's degree, in a singing group, still playing bridge and having fun with her grandchildren. By the time a doctor found the cancer, it was too late to do much. We got 2 years out of some wonder drugs and then she was gone.

I was able to be there for my mom at the end. Towards her last days, she told me that she was ready, she had no regrets, and she had done everything she wanted to do in her life. That hit me hard – because there was no way that I was going to be able to say that if my life kept going in the same direction.

After Mom died, I fell into a deep depression. With some support from family and on the advice of my wonderful therapist, I took some time off and went to the Caribbean where I fell in love with scuba diving. That and some good anti-depressants (better living through chemistry!), saved me and gave me some perspective.

I didn't accept the reorganization at my company and negotiated a really substantial severance package. After comments like "women don't belong in operations", I had a pretty good case for employment discrimination. I got everything I asked for. It gave me some breathing room to help my Dad get resettled and take some time for myself.

But I could not figure out what to do with the rest of my life. I had been thrown for a loop by two major life traumas that were not in my control. And the longest break I had taken in my life without working or going to school was 3 months at the age of 19. I now had the time AND the money. So, I took it on faith that I would find work when I was ready and went traveling with my son all over South America for 4 months.

Life is full of surprises. Returning from that first trip I still was not ready to re-enter the world of work. I went back to South America to study Spanish in Quito and travel places we missed. But the traveling part didn't happen. I met a guy. The last thing I expected (how it always happens, right?) We fell in love. I came home, sold my house and belongings and went back to live in Ecuador where we built a bed and breakfast on a beautiful beach. It was idyllic. Going back and forth for 3 years for visa reasons, I stepped back into selling real estate for extra money and was thrilled with the flexibility and freedom it gave me to come and go.

Which was a good thing, because the Ecuadorian economy did not cooperate with our dream. But my path was now clear. I married my Ecuadorian sweetheart and we landed in San Francisco 20 years ago. My real estate career gave me the ability to keep balance in my life and work independently. In 2018 we will celebrate our 20th wedding anniversary and we are happy to be home with children, grandchildren and dear friends and family. And we are eating LOTS of ice cream!

My mom's lesson was really important for me even though I didn't realize it till late in life. So I want to pass it along. Take advantage of what is in front of you, always. Enjoy your life and do the things that are important to you. When your life is ending, be able to say you have no regrets. Now is the time. Don't let your ice cream melt.

About Deborah Lopez

Just a few things to add to my story - My joy comes from my children (son, daughter + son-in-law) and grandchildren (6-year-old Hanna and a little sister on the way). My husband Jorge did not speak a word of English when we met 22 years ago but we are both bilingual now. I love selling real estate in San Francisco and have helped countless clients with both happy and difficult life transitions. I still scuba dive when I get the chance and we love to travel. Life is good and full of ice cream. I am Deborah Lopez.

Your Body Wants to Heal:
How Cancer and Chronic Illness Taught Me to Trust My Body

by Kara Sorensen

The month of my 32nd birthday was chaos, and I was forced to surrender. What came out of it was a new way of being and a new professional career: one where I learned to trust the intelligence of my body. I was called in for a next-day appointment with the chief OB-GYN. I'd been back for testing several times in the previous six months with persistent symptoms and I was hoping to finally get some answers. I remember the chair I was sitting on and how close she faced me in her tiny office. She barely introduced herself before I burst into tears. She told me I had the beginning stages of cancer. She scheduled me for her first available surgery. It was aggressive, and we needed to act fast!

After inhaling the shock, and wiping the tears, I told her about my month — how I'd just moved, how I'd been forced to fire a key employee, and how my dad was diagnosed with a terminal autoimmune disease.

It felt like the bottom dropped out, but somehow, I felt relief to learn what was going on. I was in caring hands, and I could finally let go. I felt this through the fear, panic, and uncertainty. I knew that I couldn't live my life the same way any longer. I needed to change.

My doctor put me on medical disability to prepare for surgery and to slow the stress train. What happened next set a whole new course for my personal and professional life. It brought me to the place I am now: knowing in my bones that healing is not only possible, but inevitable. Inevitable if I pursued it with gentleness, curiosity, and persistence. Sometimes, even, with reckless abandon, but always with love.

The pivotal moment in my healing journey occurred on my mom's doorstep the very same week. My mom answered a knock at the door. An acquaintance who had moved out of town felt she "needed to come by and say hello." My mom told her what was going on with me, which inspired her to give my mom a business card of someone she thought could help.

I followed the breadcrumbs. I'd seen a holistic practitioner when I was 21, so I was open to non-traditional forms of healing. My new advocate told me that I could heal this naturally and that doing so would reduce the likelihood of it recurring. To the horror of my family, I postponed my surgery and embarked on a mostly herbal protocol. My new nurse practitioner was a pioneer in an approach that is much more common today, but this was 2001. I did need a second round of holistic treatment, due to my compromised immune system, but I never did need that surgery. And I'm still clear all these years later.

While collaborating with my nurse practitioner, we discovered a second diagnosis a month later. This wasn't as shocking, as I had suspected that I had thyroid issues for over a decade, but it still brought tears. After doctors had ignored my obvious symptoms and my numerous requests for thyroid tests, I finally got the right ones. I had Hashimoto's disease. I'd had it for years. My thyroid was one-and-a-half times its normal size and scarred.

Healing from an autoimmune disease was much less straightforward than healing from cancer, and the process is much less understood by Western medicine.

I've since learned that these conditions were partly due to early childhood traumas and were exacerbated by stress.

After being on disability for a year — and still exhausted — a friend suggested that I work for an acupuncturist, who, in turn, urged me to go get my master's degree in Chinese medicine. This was another step in my healing journey. I had both my bachelor's and master's degrees in nutrition and I knew that combining these would be powerful medicine from my experience with both.

Through all of this, I have always felt that my body never fails me. She shows me the symptoms, which are the calls for healing. Sometimes I listen. Sometimes I've been so stressed out trying to survive that I ignored them and delayed getting help. I also got stuck in overwhelm as there weren't always traditional or holistic medical answers.

What I know now is that when we listen to the cries and symptoms of our body and address them with compassion and curiosity, not only can balance be restored, but our lives are much better as a result. The answers come. Sometimes, these answers circle around and keep resurfacing until we finally get it. Sometimes it takes decades, as it has for me, to finally take the right action. In these situations, it's easy to judge yourself: "Why did I wait so long?" "Why didn't I just leave that job or that boyfriend?"

But everything happens at the right time, like when the woman showed up at my mom's door or when my boss suggested I take acupuncture training. Somehow — and I can't explain it — the solutions show up when we surrender.

After all of the challenges I've faced with my health since childhood, I have felt at the end of my rope many times, yet, I love my body more than ever. I trust her. I listen to her. Through the frustration, I know it's my mind that needs the adjustment. My body is innocent.

Our symptoms, our sensations, our inner trust and knowing are what guide us to the solutions that heal us. They feel like the problem, but they are the messenger. This is how intelligence speaks. When we learn to listen and trust our body, a whole new world opens up — a world where we aren't the victim, but rather we are empowered.

Our bodies want to heal. They're always striving for wholeness, asking for it, whispering for it, begging for it, and sometimes yelling for it.

Will you listen?

About Kara Sorensen

As a Nutritionist and Body Wisdom Awakening Coach, I help women dive more deeply into the physical, spiritual, and emotional roots behind their health issues and autoimmune dis-ease. Through our work together, they learn to eat what's perfect for them, heal deeply, and tap into their joy, despite the circumstances. I'm most passionate about helping women learn to listen to, trust, and love their bodies and themselves, so that they can live their lives with unbridled health and joy.

For support on your healing journey, click the free link below:

"Love Your Body Blueprint: 5 Simple Steps to Bring Joy into Healing with Autoimmune!" www.LoveYourBodyBlueprint.com

To learn more, visit: www.KaraSorensen.com

To learn about my work with horses and healing, visit: www.UnbridledHealthAndJoy.com

Finding My True Passion and Purpose
by Tanya Lochner

I created my sixteen-year corporate career around what my definition of success was. I took my father's words to heart and literally worked day and night to be successful. The price? My health, my sanity and my soul....

I've often wondered why it takes a life changing event to connect with yourself at the deepest level and to rise above it all with a bigger transformation. Whatever the answer is, that is what it took for me and what it brought about was a life filled with Passion and Purpose I could never have imagined in my wildest dreams.

My story begins when a loving soul crossed my path at just the right time and place and refused to accept the life sentence I had succumbed to. See, I was diagnosed with an aggressive hormonal condition, adrenal hypoplasia, that would require me to be on strong medication for the rest of my life. In fact, I was handed a deadline to conceive children so that the medication could be increased. Taking hands with this unconditional and intuitive soul, I embarked on a journey of peeling away the layers of protection that was built around me. Slowly the intertwined vines of body, mind, emotions and of course soul was revealed as I faced each one with courage (and sometimes trepidation). It appears that when we are not aligned with our true nature and life's purpose, it manifests in destructive ways in other areas of our lives. The journey continued and the positive results from my holistic approach to healing were evident in more than my blood tests. Results which perplexed the endocrinologist when they tested normal without the cocktail of drugs he had prescribed. My body had undergone a transformation bigger than the excess weight that I had dropped. My outlook on life had changed and I felt hopeful for the future again despite still feeling alone in one area of my life.

A year later I had the opportunity to again shake my world to move into the next transitional phase. My career had been built and I was offered a position in a new town far away from family, friends or the supportive structures I had built around me. It was time for me to face a new world alone. I clearly remember how I fought the change and kept looking for excuses and reasons to stay. I questioned this unstoppable drive inside me to keep improving myself and going for the next goal I could fixate on. It was like trying to carve out an image in cement. Every move was painful and every day a heaviness pulling along when a different outcome didn't arrive. Until I just let go.....I surrendered to the process.

That was what happened that December when I allowed the flow of life to happen and swirl me along in its wake. I packed my bags and got on the plane, knowing there had to be reason for where I was going. What happened next feels like something out of a movie script. Within a week of arriving at my new destination I met the man of my dreams. We were married in three months and expecting our first child created in harmony and called him Levi (meaning joined in harmony). A mere ten months after he was born my daughter was conceived without us even knowing. And this little creature hid herself away for four months until we discovered her life force inside. In the scope of less than three years I had gotten almost all of my desires that I had been pining for so long. Health, love, happiness and a continuation of my life.

The next chapter unfolded when it was time to let go of my corporate career to step into my own feminine power. Finding the voice that was truly mine while becoming a mother and birthing a new business. I had to learn how to find strength in being a woman with a message to share with the world. A far cry from my masculine knowledge and expertise in a man's world. I believe I have found the center of my universe where my soul is lit up. I have found what makes my soul blossom and shine. I welcome this new chapter of growing and learning as I go deeper into uncovering what my soul's purpose is for the here and now.

Would I have done anything different looking back? I probably have a million alternatives running through my brain. Through all of my experiences though, I have come to one conclusion. These things happen to us for a reason. We grow and learn through each experiencing, making life a rich well of expansion for us. The only thing I would change is how I enjoyed the journey. I would feel more gratitude and stop wishing for the final destination to arrive. I will now continue exploring this beautiful life, looking for the fullness of each moment and feeling present, connected gratitude, with the fresh innocence like a child. Nothing describes my conclusion of life like the words of TS Elliot-

"We shall not cease from exploration, and the end of all our exploring will be to arrive where we started and know the place for the first time."

About Tanya Lochner

Tanya Lochner is a Passion and Purpose-filled Mom Strategist supporting women globally to reconnect to their own passion and purpose, while being a natural Supermom.

Natural Mama to three incredible humans and four fur kids, she lives in beautiful Cape Town, aptly known as the Mother City of South Africa. Her passion for helping women powerfully navigate life and motherhood, blossomed when she took the leap of faith in leaving her sixteen-year corporate career as a specialist and mentor, to follow her dream of working from home and being a more present mom to her own children. Infusing a holistic approach in coaching, she brings together her background in psychology, nutrition and finance to help women create a life they truly LOVE living.

Free gift: 5 Day Rocking Mama Challenge

Learn how to overcome any challenge in5 Days!

Ditch the OVERWHELM so you can live your ultimate life of Passion & Purpose

Create more TIME so you can cherish the moments with your children rather than trying to cope

Get the extra SUPPORT so you can have healthy, happy and connected children

Become a Rocking Mama here >>> http://bit.ly/5rockingmama

Courage Is Not the Absence of Fear...
by Sweeney Mae Montinola

I did not want to move to America. I was 16 when my parents received the official approval from the US embassy, a process that took more than four years. I begged my parents to let me stay one more year so I could graduate with high school friends that I grew up with but they didn't approve.

I arrived in Seattle in July of 1999. Finally reunited with my parents after four years. My parents planned a few road trips to places I only used to see on recorded VHS movies. We went to Las Vegas, San Francisco, Hollywood and San Diego. My initial disappointment slowly dissipated in time.

I was very anxious about school. After taking placement tests and submitting my transcript, it was determined that I had sufficient credits to start as a senior, but the school district decided it was best to place me as a sophomore. We did not have middle schools in the Philippines and they believed that I needed time to get acclimated to the American school system to prepare for college. I was not happy with the thought of being demoted to sophomore year.

I still feel embarrassed every time I think back to my first day of school. My mom dropped me off and I (do not want to admit) was on the verge of tears. I had pent up disappointments that started to well up into tears. I felt my face get warmer as I walked further into the hallway. I looked back and saw my mom's silhouette getting smaller and I did my best not to let those tears come. I was too old to cry on the first day of school.

Afraid to start anew, my worries started to eat me up inside. I was worried my English was not good enough. Worried that I cannot find the right words to respond if teachers call on me. It was a nerve-wracking day. I sat in the back of all my classes. I was afraid to speak to anyone. I managed to say hello to some people by lunchtime, but I tried to remain invisible for the most part.

At last, the (long) day ended at 3 pm and my mom was there to pick me up. On our way to the car, she saw posters for a dance squad try out at 6 pm. I was a cheerleader back in the Philippines and she was convinced that I needed to do this. I was afraid that I was not going to be able to catch on with their "American" dance moves. I barely wanted to speak to people. My mom did not take no for an answer.

The audition went surprisingly well! Their dance moves were easier than I thought. Too easy, actually. I should not have doubted myself, as I've always been a good dancer. We practiced immediately the following day as the first performance was at the end of that week during the first pep rally. At practice, they asked me to just observe because they were still finishing the choreography. When they were ready to show me the steps, they were shocked that I've already learned the entire routine on my own. They gave me all kinds of praises and high fives. It was the first time I ever felt good about myself since the big move to America.

Another great moment I had that week happened after our first performance. People went out of their way to say I did a good job. I stood a little taller after that performance. This gave me enough confidence boost to start sitting in the front of the class. It felt good to know that I don't have to be invisible.

A month later, I received five "student of the month" awards and continued to excel as one of the top students in school. I was elected dance co-captain the following year and elected as an ASB officer amongst other leadership positions in multiple organizations and clubs. As it turns out, they were right to make sure I had enough time to build myself up for college. I continued to excel academically and hold leadership positions through my college years.

These were important defining moments of my life. I have not since allowed fear to paralyze my possibilities. It helped me realize that fear is only in our imagination partly due to all the things we see in life or television. We tend to imagine all possible worst-case scenarios and drive ourselves mad. It's critical to practice how to channel our insecurities and concentrate on our performance. I am so lucky to have learned and realized these lessons early on. My defining moments in high school have helped shape me to be a courageous risk taker. I now find it exciting to move to a new city or to travel by myself. I moved to Los Angeles in 2009 without any definite plans. Eight years later, I am proud to have won several awards as a Marketing Director, assume multiple leadership roles as well as own my business as a marketing coach, speaker and event producer.

Fear is a process. First, it will make you feel vulnerable. Then, it may paralyze you but you must fight to realize that the negative outcomes are all in your imagination. In reality, you really have no idea of what the outcome will be. Take a deep breath and do something bold to outweigh fear's influence in your imagination. Nothing happens until you take action. It's up to you, not your imagination, to get the results you want.

I am not fearless. As women, we often read about encouragements that promote fearlessness. It's impossible to erase fear. Fear does have its place in our lives. Unless you have a magic ball that can tell the future, it's safe to say that you have no clue (ZERO!) on what the exact outcome would be. All you may be sure of are different possibilities and consequences of your action. The biggest consequence, though, of letting fear paralyze you is regret.

If the fear of failure were completely absent, I would not have built enough courage to strive for success. It helps to surround yourself with people (like my mom) who believe in you more than you do in yourself. Transform your fears into courage. It only takes one (maybe two at most) defining moments for you to realize how good it feels to overcome your fears. You become more audacious every time you overcome your fears. So go and be audacious!

About Sweeny Mae Montinola

SWEENEY MAE MONTINOLA is a multi-award winning Marketing Director for SouthBay Pavilion, a regional shopping center located in Carson CA. Sweeney has a broad range of experience in retail marketing, fashion, and event production. Her expertise includes creative marketing solutions, community relations, and social media marketing.

Active within the community, Sweeney Mae has served (or currently serving) as President of the Carson Gardena Dominguez Rotary Club, Board Member of the Gardena Carson YMCA, Board Member of the Carson Station Sheriff Support Foundation, VP of Communications for the Women's Business Council of Long Beach, Vice Chair of the City of Carson Public Relations Commission and guest lecturer at California State University, Dominguez Hills and the local Chambers of Commerce.

Sweeney Mae holds a B.A. in Marketing from Washington State University and a CMD (Certified Marketing Director) designation from ICSC (International

Council of Shopping Centers). She was previously employed by Macy's Northwest and Expedia Inc. Follow her on Instagram @sweeney_mae to stay up-to-date with her offers and speaking schedules.

Mirror, Mirror

by Wendee Neilson

Chronic illness SUCKS!

Mirror, Mirror on the wall, who's the ugliest one of all...

Mirror, Mirror on the wall, who's the biggest loser of them all...

That was how I felt living with chronic illness and later the mental and emotional abuse I endured from a sibling.

I won't lie, I will not sugar coat it to make it sound all flowery and pretty. It wasn't. I share my story not to get sympathy, but to let other women know they are not alone. Living with chronic illness is a lonely place to be. It pretty much robbed me of 15 years of my life that are gone LOST, forever...

Those years that I battled my illness were some of the darkest moments I had ever lived. As a result of bouncing from doctor to doctor, from specialist to specialist, it completely wiped out my savings. However, I choose to now look at this time lost as a gift. It was a gift because I lived life without slowing down. I had my own medical billing business that I loved but took on some clients that sucked the life out of me. It was the beginning of the end for me.

While I ran this business, I did not know how to slow down and not work. I was essentially a perfectionist, workaholic working 16-hour days, 7 days a week. I never once felt I was worthy of a vacation or finding the time to take off because there was always so much work to be done. I also did not trust myself to hire employees. So, what manifested were illnesses that forced me to slow down.

During this down time, I did not just stay home, sitting on my ass all day doing nothing. In fact, I went back to college and studied Psychology; I became a certified Life Coach. I graduated from Hypnosis school and other holistic type genres. Soon, the money dried up and I was plunging into darkness. My next move was the worse move of my life, I literally signed my soul over to the devil...

I accepted help from my younger sibling. I am grateful for the help, but it was literally what broke me, my spirit, my joy, my enthusiasm for life. He found ways to manipulate and control my every move. If I did not act a certain way, if I did not say the right thing, if I defied his authority, he threatened to cut me off, and he did several times until I graveled for his mercy. He verbally and mentally abused me on a daily basis. What's sad about that was he also was helping out our elderly mother who was not able to live on social security alone. He controlled me by threatening both of us. He used money as a pawn to control and manipulate us in doing what he thought we should be doing. Even when I tried to establish healthy boundaries from what I learned in coaching, he ignored those boundaries and continued to abuse the two of us.

For a few years, I had to endure my younger sibling telling me what a horrible person I was, what a loser I was, what a failure I was, and it went on and on. This sibling even had the nerve to tell our mother what a horrible mother she was. We both lived in such fear, that we had no idea at the time how to break free because we had become so dependent on this person. He especially thought I was a failure because I had not figured out how to make a million dollars. Which never was my goal, my goal was to help other women, but for him, that was just a "stupid, waste of time."

This mental and emotional abuse then triggered my depression. I felt hopeless, I felt so lost and I had no idea what I was on this planet to do. When he finally did cut off both my mom and I, I had no choice but to find a job so I could pay the mortgage. That is when I truly believe in my perseverance, my strength and courage to do what had to be done. I took back the control of my life, my story. I was not going to let someone else define me, tell me who I should be or not to be. I found the pen and I am again writing my story in how it needs to go. That was when my life began to change. That was my "A-Ha" moment. That was when I found my voice.

Mirror, Mirror on the wall...today, after so much pain and heartbreak I can finally say who I am. I am a creative, kind, caring, loving and a compassionate woman. I am smart, strong, intuitive, spiritual, curious, resourceful and a life-long learner. I am sensitive, shy, friendly and mostly a dreamer following her passions and dreams. I sometimes still take life too seriously and meditate on what is possible. Instead of seeing the cup half full or half empty, I now live life as the cup. Sometimes, we must walk through the ugly in order to get to the pretty.

For me, success isn't about the money (although, money is nice). Success has been my perseverance to never-ever give up. I may be down for a moment or two, but I have never, nor will I ever give up. When I am dead, that perhaps will be the day I give up. Success for me is my ability to keep moving forward with my dreams and my passions. So I've had to start over many, many times, I always kept moving forward despite all the constant road blocks. Success is a smile I see on a client's face when they have their A-HA moment. Success is having someone say to me, "because of you, I won't give up either.

About Wendee Neilson

I am a multi-faceted Artist, Life Coach, Hypnotherapist and Teacher. I am the Creative Director at Coaching You Forward. I help clients design a life they can be passionate about. Mastering one change at a time and helping them live their dreams. Discover - Embrace - Empower - Create...YOU!

I am offering a complimentary stress reduction hypnotherapy session via phone or Skype. You can email me at wjndesigns@yahoo.com, call 805-766-6856 or visit my website at wendeeneilson.com.

Recovery from Chemo
by Marci Crabtree

I didn't hear the doctor say, "Breast Cancer", but my sweet husband Tree did. It was the beginning of a very bad time for a woman who had just retired and was looking forward to travel, freedom, and fun.

From the surgery through the 3 months of chemotherapy I felt as if I lost everything of my person. I had suddenly become a weak, alone "little girl" in lady's body. I felt like I went from a mother of grown kids to a bald-headed child, who was weak and had lost her self-image. I could scarcely walk 20 feet to our mail box. I sat in my recliner because that was all I could muster. I couldn't "see" to read when the hot scalding tears from the chemo fell. I couldn't write, only scribble. I didn't cook nor clean house. Thank God for a house cleaner and "take-out" meals! And thank GOD for a wonderful husband who came home from work and didn't baby me. He loved me – even with my scar across my chest.

That was 20 years ago, but it took me down to a low spot. I had to crawl up and out of a dungeon that I was in, though no one else ever saw. It was a battle that raged in my mind. One day I called the American Cancer Society Hot Line number from a paper I had been given. The friendly voice told me that she was a Jewish mama from New York City and a cancer survivor. She was so sweet I blurted out my tale of woe. "I can't eat much, I have no strength, and the worst thing is I can't even add numbers!" I had retired just a year earlier from a job as an administrative assistant who had to work the department's budget, keep track of various numbers and accounts so the ability to do "math" was a part of me. "Don't worry, honey", she said reassuring me. "All that will pass, and you will be able to think and calculate and be as you were before the chemo. It will be gone just like the metallic taste in your mouth, and you will forget what you are going through." Her words gave "HOPE". Her words did not come to pass immediately nor without struggle and hard "work". I'm sure I could have stayed there in that prison. I thought I was doomed for life to being sick with pneumonia, bronchitis, and every other "bug" or illness, yet I made it through the 2nd year. Then it seemed the physical battle ended, and I was a free but lost "gal". I didn't feel confident like the mother of three great grown men or two young mothers. I felt like – nothing, numb, I guess.

There were 3 areas I had to overcome: the physically changed "new" me without hair and very thin; the mentally impaired me who hardly knew how to talk to anyone; and then my self-image that had been torn and battered even though no one could see it, I thought.

I didn't sit down and write a plan for recovery, but I knew I had to get out of the house. Trouble was, I still was weak. I couldn't shop, although bargain-hunting shopping had been my passion before all this. I couldn't sing nor even talk very loud or long, although I had been a speaker before this attack. I couldn't even talk with good friends the same. My life had been changed, even though I still had my loving husband, our lovely home, and 2 sweet granddaughters who lived in the same city. Their parents brought them (along with dinner) to our home every Sunday evening. But I needed more.

After chemo a wonderful gal from a Bible Study, Vera Vega, took me to AGLOW, a non-denominational Christian women's meeting one Saturday. I went after I was stronger, but still very weak. She took me to the front for prayer after the speaker. I do not remember the meeting nor who I met or what we ate – but I remember that prayer! Four or more gals I didn't know, gathered around me in quiet, with believing voices, and began to pray in words I'd never heard. I was not afraid. THEN, I knew I was healed! That must have been **Step 1**, up from the bottom of the hole.

I felt like my mouth was "glummed shut". It is a word I created because it exactly described how it was. I had this unseen glue [like that stuff the dentist puts in your mouth to make an impression of a tooth to be replaced). Ever tried to talk at that time? Ha! That was me. Finally, I decided to go and volunteer at Beverly Manor Recovery House. Some of the people I had seen while caroling there years before, couldn't talk or do much. Maybe they wouldn't notice that I couldn't talk.

It was scary to report for the first day to help with "arts and crafts", but the gal who was the head of it made me feel so welcome that I was eager to do the coloring or cutting paper or whatever was needed. The residents loved us. They were lonely and needed a friend. I went back weekly for a long time. **Step 2**.

After that the steps were easier. **Step 3** I became the friend, helper, and confident of our new woman pastor. I even went to church meetings with her down near Los Angeles. She somehow got me to teach Sunday School to adults; engineers and "really smart people".

Soon I joined AGLOW and became the greeter and later the secretary and finally the V.P. Later I went to an AGLOW Retreat and had words of power spoken over me. But it took years of stepping out and doing "The New". I'm still at it today!

Advice? Ask for support, then volunteer for others.

About Marci Crabtree

Marci Crabtree is a survivor. She has survived cancer, heart failure twice, falls that broke open her head, and other near fatal accidents. When asked how did she survive, she has two main reasons. #1: a GOD who cares about us as we go through tough times. Marci believed that "FAITH" in GOD is key to survival. She sees herself just holding her heart in her hand and saying, "OK Father – I can praise you here on earth or in heaven, but you know that my family needs me here, so I'd like to live on earth for a bit longer." #2: Marci believes she survives because her husband, Tree, and her family and friends support her and expect her to return to them whole and happy.

Marci has a "Let's get this done and have fun while we do it" attitude. She believes we are here on earth to help each other along the road. Our journey is unique for each of us, yet common threads of attitudes and outlooks can lead us to help each other during times of need.

"I know someone has been through cancer and needs to find a way to overcome the feeling of loss and despair that cancer treatment often leaves", she says. If cancer or some other life event has left you feeling worthless, unable to go on, read my article and see if it doesn't give you hope and a trick or two to put in your bag.   Marci is praying for all those who read her article to find strength and courage to move on, out of the dungeon and into freedom, a refreshing breeze, and new life!

The Excitement of Awareness
by Jacque Zoccoli

"Your father has died." At age 6 my life seemed changed forever. At that point I asked God, why? Why can't I attend the "father/daughter" events? Why must my mother raise me alone? Is this what life is going to be like? My answer - life altering, and truly sent by God "This is the worst your life will ever be. I will protect, guide, and love you forever."

Knowing I would never be alone, I lived in a freedom that is hard to explain. It has crafted my life of positivity and built a foundation that spiritually controls my every thought. Take what you wish of my journey.

It took me about 70 years to realize my purpose here on earth. When dining with a close friend, a spiritual soul, we uncovered something. She said, "You don't know, do you?" I of course, had no clue. She explained that I was placed on earth to change mankind in a positive way. I smiled and felt tingly and warm all over. I had dreamed it, though knew not how.

On my way home, amidst tears and chills, I understood what she meant. It became my "Excitement of Awareness" philosophy and life from then on. I never truly figured out how I got home that night, the tears, the enlightenment, the picture so vivid. . . all amazing and heaven sent.

From that moment on, grew my mantra *"My age justifies my wisdom; my developed clarity teaches the Excitement of Awareness"*. As a Networking Coach, Word of Mouth Strategist, and Global Collaborator – my plight and cause became to enlighten all in my path, to the wonders of essentially the 5 Cs. Before I begin this, one must become totally aware of oneself.

The *Excitement of Awareness* took me to looking first at myself, a thing one must do, to understand others. My core of God's love created a strong center, I built upon it. One of the things that shaped those early days, was my collection of quotes. At age 10, I visited a restaurant in Stockton, CA, where quotes were everywhere. I loved to escape into them and began building my life around them. Through them I realized my uniqueness, the blessings that come from the good, bad, and ugly experiences. I learned to apply "how can I improve this?" to bad things, and to cherish the good. I found that depression and sadness cannot exist when I apply gratitude to my day.

Early on, while in the Peace Corps in Liberia, West Africa, I learned the universal language of love. As I walked through life there, the smile upon a child's lips broke any language barrier. I learned that laughter dispels nearly any misunderstanding, and humor can defray nearly any ill will. I became aware of my personal impact as an American, a woman, and as an ambassador of peace. My self-esteem grew from here, the most precious and important part of my life.

Being confident in myself, open minded and curious, I began to become aware of the relationships needed with others. The 5Cs are here.

- **Commonality** – as we meet, what do we share? This is the building block of relationships.
- **Communication** – we need to communicate our commonalities.
- **Commit** – we then commit to working, playing, loving each other.
- **Contribute** – adding to the relationship is important.
- **Collaboration** then occurs, when we evolve through the process with an open mind, non-judgmentally, keeping our uniqueness.
- **GLOW** results – Guided Love Of Wholeness.

As I embarked upon the journey of relating to me, then to others, I ran into a precious life mentor, Patricia J. Munson. It was 1991 and I was part of her Women In Discovery weekend. Little did I know that she and I would become best friends, through her teachings. Nor did we know I would be her Executive Director of her Dimensions In Discovery. Such a both trying and rewarding journey needs to be shared.

Though much more than 7 life skills were learned, here are the 7 that might assist in your growth as well. I continue to grow from them, share them, revise my approach to them, and basically live them.

1. **Respect the Process** – life is an evolution, will continue with or without me, what you are going through will end.

2. **Go to Solution** – when anyone is blamed for wrong doing, fine, learn, then Go to Solution. Do not wallow in blame. It is a waste of time, emotion, energy.

3. **You are 100% responsible** – painful as it is, yes, your life, your thoughts, your actions are 100% yours. No one can "make" you anything without your permission. Once I realized that, I began to see that my control was so workable.

4. **Integrity drives everything** – when one can count on, belief in, and commit to – oneself, their integrity can then encompass others. Self-

integrity is the most precious. The most important part is saying what you feel deep inside. Often, "This doesn't work for me now" are the best words. Nothing more, no explanation. Works wonders.

5. **4 Rs** – when words or actions don't come to you right, often you **Resent** them. If, left untouched, the next interaction leads to **Resist**. Before long there is **Revenge**. When I stop the feelings right at the first R, and **Report with Love**. . . the entire formula collapses.

6. **Do not judge others** – of course we do, human nature. However, when we judge, then compare, we fall short. Instead of judgment – observe only. Not good, not bad, just the news.

7. **Be open to wonder, rather than closed by belief.** I love this one. It totally creates a mindset that clears my past and glorifies my future.

These 7 life's skills have served me well. I wish for you to feel empowered, free, and loved. You are exactly where you are meant to be, so feel blessed for it. May you join me in increasing love, prosperity and peace.

About Jacque Zoccoli

My 73 years of meandering through relationships and exploring cultures worldwide, have driven me to coach others to find new niches and alliances to grow. Please take advantage of my expertise with my *Clarity from Chaos* complimentary, online session. http://NetworkBuildersArizona.com and to schedule a session http://calendly.com/jacque-2/linkedin-one-on-one. Jacque@NetworkBuildersArizona.com

I leave you with – "Prefer to be open to wonder, rather than closed by belief." (Gerry Spence). I attract the abundance I need to fulfill my soul's purpose.

Section 5 - Empowered by choice

Mother Nature is in Control but I Still Choose:
by Ann Evanston

When one realizes they choose, in every situation, how you feel about living is remarkable. Everything in life is our choice. Our self-love stems from that. Choices for me have been hard and frightening, like moving to California for a boy I thought was magnificent (yet no commitment yet), or simple yet powerful choices, like growing our garden.

Our yard was destroyed when the contractors had to rebuild after the fire. As Earl would ask, "what should we do," my heart knew I wanted a garden. I have fond memories of my grandfather's lushly scented garden, and the joy he took in it. Of how my father loved to press flowers in phone books. I wanted to grow flowers and especially food.

Earl agreed. Having parents that died early in life, 53 and 61, we knew how important food was to living long, full lives. April 2018 will start out eleventh year growing our own food. The garden is 9000 square feet, high-density, organic, urban and we grow food and flowers ALL year. It has been an adventure in choices.

Dig trenches, raise beds, composting. How? Ok, raised beds, clay it too hard to dig, and composting is "dirt man's" (i.e. Earl) job. Planting and harvesting. When? Will mother nature agree? Probably not, but seasons are short. Plant high density to get the best return on investment.

A drought? Are you kidding me woman? Ok, choose to grey water. Be more sustainable. Put a damn bucket in the sink! Keep it there when the drought is "over."

Wait, why is that ONE kale plant shaking, like the wind is blowing, in that HUGE 8x4x2 box of greens? Fuck me it's a fucking mole! Dig the dirt out of all NINE boxes, ALL 64 square feet of it, times NINE boxes, put mole guard down, fill them back up.

Slugs. Snails. Aphids. Organic is hard. Pick and rub them off. Oh my look at that, we attract Monarchs! I was going to dig out all that milkweed, choose to leave it. And that is a huge praying mantis! Organic is paying off.

Summer. Harvest cucumbers, zucchini, beans, corn, and peppers. Holy tomato! They are in abundance this year! We didn't grow them to compost them or give them all away. Learn to can. Pickle. Freeze. Wow, that's just one weeks' worth of canning!

Winter. Harvest greens, cabbage, beets, carrots, choys, celery. Wow did it just get THAT warm in February? The bok choy is bolting. Learn to ferment. Make kimchi.

Be ready to do that WHEN the plants say it's time. Be willing to share with those that appreciate.

"Hey friend, want something from the garden since we are coming over?"

"Sure, how about some zucchini?"

"That doesn't grow this time of year."

"Oh, I never thought of that, we buy it all year at the grocery."

Choose to eat seasonally.

Yes, I choose. In every situation. Big or small. Hard or easy. Having this garden has shown me that I can, at any given moment choose. I can choose overwhelm, stress, frustration. I can choose adventure, learning, creativity. Hard or easy is also a choice. But the state of not choosing will eat away at our soul. Make a choice: left or right; fat or thin; stay or go, love or leave. And then BE in that choice. Just like the stories in this section, these women have had to make choices, some so very scary- and with choice they are truly living a thriving life. Just like me and my garden.

And One Last Bit About Ann

Ann M. Evanston is a wife, leader, lover and creator. Manifesting the "Unscripted Stories" eBook series all stemmed from her love for people and their stories. Her abundant thinking transcends everything she does....even her tomatoes! EVERY person, has a story, even one as simple as growing a garden can make others laugh, inspire and change others' lives! Become a part of the unscripted community on Facebook! Her passion is showing strong women how to live fully in self-love. She loves connecting:

Facebook
LinkedIn
Twitter
YouTube
Website

The Center Slice of the Tomato: by Kerry Hargraves

My husband and a tomato taught me a very valuable lesson about living a bodacious life. I'm pretty sure that wasn't what he meant to do but lessons show up in interesting disguises.

We were working together in the kitchen, collaborating on a couple of sandwiches. As I was slicing the big, ripe, beefsteak tomato he pointed out I should be slicing it so that we would each get a center slice.

Now this may not be a revelation to anyone else, but prior to that moment I would have started slicing at one end and used the slices as they came. And I would put the best of those on his sandwich. Then I would have bagged up the rest of the tomato and put it in the fridge to be used for the salad or whatever came next. It wouldn't have occurred to me to take the best slices for both of us.

That got me wondering. Where else am I missing the juiciest, best, yummiest experiences. And more importantly, why?

The why is both simple and complicated. I was raised like so many other girls, to share, to put others first, to avoid appearing selfish, certainly not to be greedy or self-centered. Things had to be divided evenly and if they weren't the bigger portion was given to the other person.

Other people's comfort came first. Other people's needs were to be met before my own. If someone else wanted the last buttercream frosting rose on my birthday cake, they got to have it. That's what well raised, proper little girls did.

But you know what? I'm not a little girl now. I'm a grown-ass woman! If it's my birthday cake and I want the last rose I'm damn well going to take the last rose. (Hmm...maybe I need to address some unresolved resentments over birthday cake decorations.) Now, if it's your cake I'll ask for it and I won't be offended if you say "no."

Shortly thereafter we were eating at our favorite prime rib restaurant. Prior to the tomato revelation I would have started by eating the outer edges of the prime rib and when full, leaving the tender center piece to come home in a doggy bag. While the dog never saw a bite of the leftovers somehow, I seldom did either. I routinely saved the best part in case someone else wanted it.

This time I went straight for center. Any left overs were now the less desirable parts (still delicious though.) I've approached every meal this way ever since.

I bet, especially if you're a parent or loving spouse, you are not in the habit of taking the best parts for yourself. I challenge you to consider this. Why shouldn't you?

I admit I still struggle with this. When preparing a meal and one piece of fish is done a little better than another, or one bowl of ice cream is bigger than the other my first impulse is to give the "better" one to my husband. Why? Because to do otherwise is what; selfish, greedy? And good girls are never selfish or greedy. But wait…I'm the one doing the work. I did the cooking and clean up. I disturbed the sleeping cat to get up from my nice comfortable recliner to serve the ice cream. He could but he doesn't. So why shouldn't I keep the better one occasionally?

I figure I got it right when I can't remember which one was the "better" one by the time I serve it but that's beside the point. The point is I am, you are, every bit as entitled to the best as anyone else. You are worth it.

So, take the center slice of the tomato. Eat the best part of the steak. Keep the bigger bowl of ice cream. Eat the last of the Girl Scout cookies when he isn't home. Doesn't he do that to you, or is that only at my house?

About Kerry Hargraves

www.KerryHargraves.com

I'm an artist, author, explorer and retired business owner. Mostly though, I am curious. I LOVE figuring out why people act that way. I LOVE taking things apart to figure out how they work and how to fix them. I LOVE new technologies and gadgets and discovering how to help others use them more creatively.

Funny thing though (OK, maybe not so funny, it's just the damn truth) I am done trying to do something because someone says I should! And I have earned the right to live playfully and messily.

Decisions Under Stress: by Julieanne Case

Detours in life are a given. Some are startling with the rapidity at which they show up. A great example is a wildfire. After three weeks of glamping in our kitchen, due to a red-tagged Wolf range, our new stove finally arrived on Monday, December 4. And amazingly, the three major hurdles to get it installed were dispatched with relative ease and our stove was installed. We even got to use it that night.

After dinner, I was on the computer and my husband had gone into the bedroom. I was chatting with a friend and we lost electricity. I quickly turned off the computer to prevent any damage from a power surge when the electricity returned. It came on and went out again. I gave up and decided to sit by the bay window. Our house looked south and I could see west from the window as well. When I looked out to the west, I saw the largest, blackest form with a voluminous head on it. It looked Godzilla like with a huge head and a long body. I knew it was not a good sign. I kept looking out and it seemed to be getting bigger. I heard there was a fire in Santa Paula, but that was a distance away and to the east of us. But something was niggling at me. I decided I was going to change into warmer clothes. It was very windy, and it was a cold wind. Before I did, I told my husband that I thought he should get dressed; it didn't look good. He just waved me away.

After changing, I looked for some small luggage and large baskets or canvas bags. I was almost finished changing when I heard pounding on our door and our neighbor said, "Prepare to evacuate." We were under mandatory evacuation due to a fire coming from over the mountain behind us. At that moment, my clear thinking went and so did every bit of saliva in my mouth. I kept drinking water, but I couldn't get my mouth wet. I put things in my bags, but it was now haphazard. I got some things and forgot other things that I would come to need. I couldn't decide what to take either. My thinking was a complete jumble at that point.

I'm an avid photographer, and I have thousands of pictures. I also have lots of photos that were my mom's. I had salvaged my mom's photos from a fire that took her life. I couldn't believe this was happening and I didn't have enough time to process this or enough room in the cars to put all the photos. Would they survive this time? I am an oil painter. Many of my paintings had been in a gallery, but now, most of my paintings were in my house and I had no way to save them all. What do I take? How many? It didn't matter. No room in the cars. There were already things in the car that took up room.

I asked Ron about whether I should take the poppies, a three-by-four-foot painting that had won several awards. He said it would get ruined in the car. We had a few more minutes and I remembered to get some backup disks. I remembered some cash in a drawer. Then I found a way to accept walking away from the paintings. I had pictures of them. They wouldn't be completely lost and I could get them printed on canvas, called giclées, if I should lose them. However, there was one painting that I was working on and it wasn't done yet. In fact, it hadn't quite come alive yet. So, I decided to take that painting with me because it needed a chance to come alive.

I could get this painting in the car. I realized that I would have to be content with what photos I had stored on the backup disks, on Facebook, and what I had moved to the Cloud. I could drive away at that point. I didn't know if we would see our house again.

Then I also realized that our new stove had just arrived that day! No way to pack that either. At least we had a chance to christen it that night before the mad dash.

Our home did survive. There was quite a bit of ash all around our house. Some of it got into the house, even when it was all buttoned up. Now we have to look at cleaning up the fallout from the fire.

I saw a quote recently that really resonated with me.

> Even though there are days I wish I could change some things that happened in the past, there's a reason the rear-view mirror is so small and the windshield so big, where you're headed is much more important than what you've left behind.

I realized that the photos represent where I've been, what I've seen. It's true for the oil paintings too. I could create new paintings from a more accomplished me if I needed to do so. If I keep looking at the past, I might miss what is in front of me. How much time do we spend looking back? Does it benefit us? I need to look out the windshield more and spend less time looking back!

∴

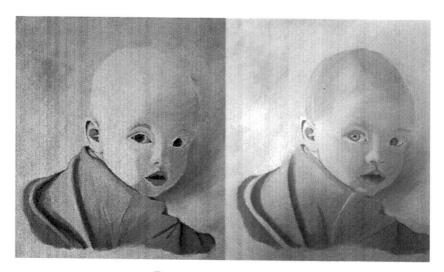

BEFORE AND AFTER THE FIRE

About Julieanne Case

http://julieannecase.com

Julieanne Case came from a left brained world, having been a computer programmer who worked on the Apollo mission that landed on the moon. Due to circumstances orchestrated by God/Universe/Source, she joined the growing ranks of the right brained world starting in 2001. She became an energy healing practitioner in 2004 and has studied various techniques. She is a Reconnective Healing Practitioner, an Intuitive Healing Artist, and a blogger. Her paintings are filled with amazing healing frequencies, light and vibrancy. She also teaches art and Drawing on The Right Side of the Brain. She assists you in rekindling the child within that leads to your creativity and your joy! We each have a Creative Soul inside. It's time to awaken it to bring about your best you!

Live
by Karlyn Davis-Welton

"Gaze upon the wondrous blessings you have in the here and now.

For if you will cultivate His peace in your heart today, you will be able to cultivate that same peace in others."

- Your beloved Jaybird, 2-14-2013

Our journey in life is a compilation of chapters in a book. The pages within each chapter are filled with stories of all the moments in which we lived. These moments are a testament of our life. Yet, as we go about our days, weeks, months, years…are we really living the life we want to live, or do we allow life's distractions to get in the way? I wonder if too often when given an opportunity to break from the daily grind, do we give way to the normal patterns of our lives? Do we get so caught up in the whirlwind of our daily routines, time tables, and to-do lists…that we forget what is really important in life — our relationships and the possibilities of new ones?

Once in a lifetime, you meet the one who makes your life come alive. God gave him to me knowing that I would love him beyond reason. On November

17, 2001, my precious Jaybird walked into my life, forever changing every aspect of my life. I had waited a long time to find that special someone who would love me unconditionally—someone who would understand me and love me like no other, would be my greatest advocate, and encourage me to fulfill my life's dreams. The day he walked through that door, my life suddenly became full of meaning and purpose. Oh, how I wanted to grow old with him.

In a fleeting moment, my life came to an unforeseen halt. I was faced with the incredible gut-wrenching decision to take the love of my life off his ventilator, a compassionate decision that would forever alter the story of my life.

It was around noon on November 27, 2016 when the team removed the ventilator. Our dearest friends and family were with us. We sang hymns, read scriptures, and played our favorite songs, including our wedding song, "Hero" by Enrique Iglesias. I was unusually calm. I focused only on him, fully aware of the significance of our last moments together. These would be permanently etched in my heart and mind. I realized there wasn't much time.

Suddenly, my Jaybird's eyes flew open.

Eyes opening wider and wider,

He was seeing our heavenly place of eternity.

One eyebrow raised up,

I watched as relief washed across his face.

His eyes focused.

And, looked right at me,

Into me.

I showered him with kisses.

No more pain, my love.

Go to Him.

I promise to be brave.

Three more breaths.

He mouths,

I love you,

Over and over again.

Another kiss,

As I held him in my arms.

I felt his soul slipping away.

One last kiss.

His final breath 1:49 p.m.

I gently closed each eye,

Sealing each one with my lips.

I then kissed his forehead and his lips one last time.

I love you my Jaybird,

Always and forever.

See you later,

din vackra kärlek

The saddest part is when the person who gave you the best moments in life suddenly becomes a memory. Fifteen years wasn't long enough. However, sometimes the person we desire to fill the pages in our book of life are only meant to be a chapter. As I move forward in my grief, I choose to live because that is what my Jaybird wanted. It is what I want, too. I embrace each moment of my day—striving to be brave, even during the painful moments, when grief washes over me and takes my breath away. I choose to slowly and gently move through my grief, allowing myself to feel the pain, to bring healing.

My Jaybird taught me a valuable lesson—to live. To embrace my life whole-heartedly and to truly focus on the ones I love so dearly. Our future will always be unknown to us. The past will always have the potential to fill our hearts with strife. Yet, in the present, we may sit and find everlasting peace and contentment. For if we cultivate peace within ourselves, we will cultivate that same peace in others.

If you are grieving, have lost great love, don't forget to live.

The day my beloved walked into my life marked a time of great change filled with courage, strength, and love. It also signified a poignant moment of letting go. This is also true as the chapter ended far too soon. This will always be my favorite chapter in my life. I can't wait to see my Jaybird again. But for now,

I have many pages yet to be written in my book of life. For now, I will turn the page and close this chapter, moving forward in my journey through life. This is my legacy.

About Karlyn Davis-Welton

Karlyn Davis-Welton--author, K-12 educator/teaching coach and professor, painter, and philosopher—is currently completing her doctorate in education. Her work has appeared in *The Reading Teacher*, among other professional educational journals. She devotes her current research to giving voice to 3-5 grade mathematical educators, who are shifting their teaching to student-centered methodologies, especially with English language learners and other under-served students. Karlyn is also at work on her memoir, *He Lifts Me Up*, in which she explores her experiences of grief and loss while struggling to fulfill her promises to herself and to her late husband (departed from this earth 11/27/2016).

karlyn.daviswelton@gmail.com

A Pivotal Life Changing Decision
by Eilis Philpott

This story is about a decision I made many years ago and as the title suggests it was a decision had a major impact on the rest of my life.

Before I share what the decision was and what I chose, let me give you a little background information. I grew up in Ireland the eldest of 9 children. I was a very sensitive child but back then, in Ireland, there was no reference for this. I was perceived as shy and told that I needed to learn how to speak up for myself. I had irrational fears and was very introspective. I had periods of depression which went undiagnosed and became more frequent and more severe as I got older.

The first time I was hospitalized I was in my early 20's and was suffering from severe depression and anxiety. I was either crying non-stop or having major panic attacks. Again, in Ireland back then, it was not generally recognized that you could get treatment for what I was going through. I thought I was going crazy. I was told I needed to pull myself together, give myself a kick in the pants and go get a job. When I was eventually hospitalized I was diagnosed with reactionary depression which meant that I was reacting to a number of major traumatic events which had occurred over the previous year. I was given various medications and over the period of about 3 months I started to feel better (for the first time in many years). I was sent home, still highly medicated, and told to get on with my life. My doctor also told me that I would never be able to have a stressful job and to give up any thoughts of pursuing teaching. (I had been studying science education at the time.)

A few years passed and with each new stressor new medications were added to my regime. I got engaged and moved to London to be with my fiancé. When I went to fill my prescriptions for the medications I had been prescribed I was told that a lot of them were blacklisted in the UK and should not be used in the combinations that I had been taking them. Needless to say, the move caused a major relapse, which resulted in my being admitted to a psychiatric hospital in London.

At the hospital in London my meds were assessed, changed and I started therapy. My therapist, Jenny, allowed me to feel. She helped me see that what I was experiencing was real and that I needed love and support. I started feeling emotions and uncovering why I was feeling what I was feeling. For the first time I did not have to repress my emotions.

Let's quickly take a step back about two years to a different move to London. I had found a flat and a job within a few days. Everything seemed fine and appeared to be going well but inside I was not doing well. My depression and anxiety were becoming unbearable and I felt I had nowhere to turn. I ended up going back to Ireland to my family home and feeling a complete failure.

This second time in London was excruciating and my default option was to go back to Ireland. My body was so anxious that it would constantly be jerking, and I was afraid to go anywhere or do anything. I was also going back and forth between actually staying in London this time or whether to return to Ireland. I had been there a short time, was taking the new meds, and having regular therapy when one morning I was scheduled for a therapy session at 11am. Everything seemed to be the same as usual and then Jenny said *"We are not continuing this therapy session. It is ending right now, and you have until 1pm today to decide whether you are going to stay in London or go back to Ireland. Once the decision is made you are committed to it. If you choose to stay it will be a long, hard and painful journey but it will be worth it"*.

My mind was in a whirl! I knew that if I went back to Ireland I would never leave, that I would be stuck in my family home with my parents and never live my own life as an independent adult. I also knew that if I chose to stay and heal I would have to face a lot of very painful emotions that I had not previously dealt with. I was also afraid that I would never actually feel well and that I was taking a huge risk if I chose to stay. I was also realizing that I really did not know myself and I was in London with the man I was planning to marry. What if that didn't work out either.

I'm sure you can imagine the turmoil I was in. It may seem like an obvious choice but remember I was in a bad way. It was nearly impossible for me at that time to live a so called normal life. I was afraid to do everything, I was constantly in despair and having panic attacks.

At 1pm, I met Jenny in the therapy room and told her that I had come to a decision. I had decided to stay. It was the best decision I ever made. Looking back now many years later I can see the enormity of that decision. This was not just a fork in the road, it was the most important decision I ever made. It was pivotal and life changing. If I had gone back to Ireland I can see now that I would never have gotten well, and my future would have been bleak.

So, I stayed.

I'm not denying that it was hard, it was very hard. I was in the hospital for 6 months, but I got off all my medication and continued with therapy. In the transition period between leaving the hospital for good and living life independently I worked part time and began to get my confidence back. I went back to school and completed a Post Graduate qualification in Education. I got a job as a High School Science Teacher (remember the doctor's in Ireland said I could never do that). This was a huge step for me and vindicated how far I had come.

I'm not saying that life was easy and that I didn't stumble and have set backs along the way. What I am saying is despite these setbacks and life situations happening and that when confronted with some other major trauma in my life, I never ended back in a psychiatric hospital. I have continued to work on myself since then, moving from traditional therapy to alternative healing modalities and energy healing. I became a practitioner and have been supporting others now to move forward in their life with love and joy.

After reading my story what I want you to know, from the core of your being, is that no matter how low you feel, no matter how bleak life may seem and no matter what anyone tells you, you can make it. You can rise above your perceived limitations, you can grow and thrive, you can uncover your personal truth and not only make it but live with joy, purpose and love. I did it, so can you!

Oh, and I married the guy, I went through hell and back too, lol!

About Eilis Philpott

Eilis is the owner of Soul Healing Journey, LLC and has been a healing practitioner for 20+ years.

Eilis is a certified Soul Language Practitioner, a certified Rebirther, and is a certified in Akashic Field Therapy. She is a Reiki Master in Usui/Raku-kei Reiki and Angelic Reiki and has received extensive training in many other healing modalities.

She helps people understand who they are at a soul level. Using various modalities she supports them in clearing those patterns that are preventing them from expressing themselves at that core level. With this healing Eilis' clients can attain a level of deep peace that they have not experienced in this lifetime.

As well as individual sessions (in person and remotely), Eilis also offers group classes, workshops and events.

Website is www.soulhealingjourney.com

Finding My Voice
by María Tomás-Keegan

November in New England can be unpredictable. Warm and sunny one day—grey, socked-in and blustery the next. My life was just like that—New England weather: just wait a minute and it will change.

I remember the leaves were a brilliant burgundy, gold and orange in the rising sun. I wasn't feeling so brilliant. I was trying to be quiet as I got ready for work. I didn't want to wake him. Last night he said awful things to me and, as hard as I tried not to, what came out of my mouth was hurtful, too. I wanted to leave before anything more could be said.

It wasn't the first time. I honestly lost count how many times this had happened before. It had been going on for so long that the pit in my stomach took up permanent residence. The lump in my throat caused my voice to quiver, my hands trembled, and tears were never far away. I was beginning to recognize how unpredictable he had become. I was living scared.

As I came out of the master bedroom, ready to head down the stairs to the garage, he came from the kitchen with a threatening voice, "Where do you think you're going?" I stopped, still with my back to him. I didn't answer. He yelled it again. I turned around and he was standing right in front of me holding my favorite chef's knife in his hand, pointed right at my chest. A blood-curdling scream came out of me like never before.

He dropped to his knees and dropped the knife. He started to sob. It was as though he was a different man when holding the knife. His eyes were wild and angry. The rage in his voice frightened me. I had seen and heard it before, but I had no idea what that man was capable of until that morning.

From his knees, he begged forgiveness. For the first time ever, the tears did not come. The pit in my stomach was surely there and my voice quivered, and my hands shook. But this time, it felt different. This time I was angry—not scared. I walked out the front door and went to my neighbor's home to call the police.

Then the tears came—uncontrolled. And the questions—why am I on this roller coaster of emotions? How long will I continue to give in to him? What's wrong with me?

This was my second marriage. My first husband cheated on me. My second husband was abusive. And I was afraid to be that woman who was divorced twice. Plus, I was afraid to live alone—I had never been totally alone before. Yet I had this amazing career at which I was in total control and confident.

Who is this woman? How can she immerse herself in work, get rave reviews from clients and management alike and direct a staff who respects her great leadership style, while she is quaking in her shoes to go home and be alone with her thoughts?

I felt comfortable with the corporate me—I was somehow able to set aside my personal turmoil. Every morning before leaving home I would stand in front of the mirror, take a deep breath, review my business calendar and put on a mask, figuratively speaking, so I could get through the day pretending that my life was just fine. Often, I would find things to do after work to delay the inevitable loneliness and soul-crushing reality that awaited me at home.

The weekends were the worst. Too much time on my hands—to think, to relive and to regret. I pushed my family and friends away because I didn't want to talk about it. I stopped doing the creative projects that I loved because I just didn't feel creative anymore. I stayed stuck in that place for what seemed like a long time.

Little did I know that it's that kind of time that can start the healing process when it's used to one's advantage. A dear friend, who felt pushed away, knocked on my door one Saturday and asked me when I was going to start living again, and could she be a part of it.

It was an awakening for me—I realized that I was barely coping. I invited her in and we talked for hours. She gave me some ideas. I decided to put them into action.

202

The first thing I did was research to find a coach or therapist. With her help, I became aware of a pattern in my thinking and a behavior that led me to hide from many of the traumas in my life. Being molested as a child and blaming myself; being a young caregiver for my aunt who died and blaming myself; being cheated on and blaming myself; being abused ...

Awareness is such a gift. Choice is another. Once I saw the pattern of blame and recognized the behavior of throwing myself into my career to hide from the emotions I didn't want to feel, I chose to feel again. It wasn't pretty at first, for sure. I spent the better part of a week hiding as I read self-help books, went to therapy sessions and cried till my eyes swelled shut. Then I felt safer to open up and let my family and friends who love me back into my life. I shared with them and cried some more.

I still put the mask on to get through the day at work, but soon I was able to control the emotions with empowering self-talk (one of the books I read), so I could be myself without the mask. Funny how people noticed a change — the smile was more real, and the eyes smiled too. I was feeling more relaxed. That pit in my stomach finally went away. My hands lost their tremble and I found my voice again.

About Maria Tomas-Keegan

María Tomás-Keegan spent 30 years in Corporate America, juggling her career and her life transitions. Even strong, successful women can get derailed when life happens. From divorce, caring for loved ones, career changes, relocations, being laid-off and early retirement she learned first-hand how to take off the mask and move beyond coping and surviving.

Today, María is founder of *Transition & Thrive with Maria* where she is a Life Transition Coach for women. She shares her life with heart-mate, Jim, and four fur-babies, Harley & Maverick, Bailey & Kharma.

María's program, *Thrive for Life*, is available via workshop, DIY online, group and private coaching. For more information, her free book and links to her newsletter and video interview series called *Tips for the Transition*, please visit: www.TransitionAndThriveWithMaria.com

Confessions of a Fit Girl
by Jonelle Boyd

229. As I looked down at the scale those were the numbers that stared back at me, hitting me like a ton of bricks. I knew I was overweight... at 25 years old I'd been overweight all my adulthood and the majority of my life, but 229 pounds?!? Sure, I liked to eat... I liked to eat a lot... and sure, I was wearing a size 18, heading towards a 20, that was one of the reasons why I'd given up on shopping anywhere but plus size stores... but 229 POUNDS?!? HOW DID THIS HAPPEN? Reality is, how it happened was no longer the issue, but how to lose the weight was.

Always a big eater, I'd been overweight since I was 12, but with heart palpitations and the reality of being over 200 pounds while standing only 5ft. 3 inches tall, I knew I had to do something. It wasn't easy, but I started walking for exercise, making healthier eating choices and cutting my portions. It was a slow and steady process, each month losing 1-3 pounds. By the end of one year I'd lost 22 pounds! I felt good about the weight loss, but the process was going a little slower than I would have liked. Realizing that I may need a little help, I decided to try a popular weight loss program that would deliver meals to my home. My goal was to get down to 150 pounds and fit into a size 10.

The first week on the program garnered some amazing results, I lost 5 pounds! Those results were enough to keep me faithful to the program, and with exercise, I lost an average of 1-3 pounds a week. Fast forward to 10 months later and I met my goal: 150 pounds, a size 10! But it didn't stop there! While the weight loss program gave me my start, I started learning about nutrition on my own. And never being the type of girl who liked sports, gym class, or anything remotely close to exercising, I now LOVED to exercise! Go figure!

AFTER PIC – JUNE 23, 2012;
MY WHOLE BODY FITS IN ONE LEG OF MY OLD SIZE 18 PANTS!

So that sounds like that should be the end of my story. *"And she lived happily ever after. The End"*, right? Wrong! While there have been ups, there have also been downs. First let's start with the actual weight itself. At my lowest I was 126 pounds. I cannot tell you how amazing it felt to know that I had actually lost over 100 pounds!!! I was riding high and feeling great about myself! But that doesn't mean that everyone around me felt the same way. The comments I began receiving turned from *"Wow! You look great!"* to *"You don't need to lose any more weight, you're getting too skinny!"* I'll admit, I was thin, but nowhere near the point to cause for concern. And if it wasn't comments judging me on my weight, now what I was choosing to eat was being scrutinized. *"What are you eating?!?"* *"That looks disgusting!"* *"I'd rather be fat and enjoy what I'm eating than to eat that!"* Wow! How rude can you get, right? But all of these comments were becoming everyday occurrences. What I began to realize that I didn't know at the time was that those type of negative comments were jealousy. Not necessarily jealousy regarding my looks, but rather of my determination and the fact that I had done something all of my rude commenters, a.k.a – "haters", were never able to do: set a goal, work hard to achieve it, and actually accomplish it. It took me awhile, but I finally understood that the problem lied within them, not me.

206

After a couple of years of riding high from my weight loss success somehow, I managed to get back up to 170 pounds again. How? Well, I could blame it on a number of things... stress from my job... stress from the "haters"... no time to cook... I could blame it on all of these things and honestly, I'd be right because that's life! In other words, how did I gain almost 50 pounds? Life happened. As I like to say, being fat happens. Let me explain.

Health conscious people talk a lot about eating healthy, exercising and being fit, but sometimes I think the average person might get the impression it's wrong or shameful to be fat. Well, I'm here to tell you that being fat happens. It happened to me and it's happened to countless of others. I am well aware that there are many different reasons how or why it happens, but regardless of what those reasons may be, you have absolutely nothing to be ashamed of. Am I proud that once allowed myself to get to reach nearly 230 pounds? No. But I am proud that I made the decision to change my life? Yes. All it takes is the courage to decide to do something different.

Which brings me to my last point: it takes courage to do this thing! People don't realize until after they begin their own journey just how much guts it takes... resisting food temptation...beginning an exercise program when maybe you've never exercised a day in your life... dealing with the unwanted opinions & comments from the haters who are sure to come... all of this takes courage. And I'm a living witness that it's all in you! All you have to do is take that first step and never look back!

Fast forward to today and I am at a weight and size that I'm comfortable with and can easily maintain. My love for fitness & nutrition has continued to thrive, with me becoming a Certified Personal Trainer in 2013. The best part of this whole journey is that losing weight not only changed me on the outside, but the inside as well, increasing my self-esteem and giving me a bigger push to motivate and encourage others. As long as you have faith, work hard, and stay determined, ANYTHING IS POSSIBLE!

CURRENT PIC – SEPTEMBER 2, 2017

About Jonelle Boyd

Jonelle Boyd is a User Experience/Interface Web Designer in her mid-30s, residing in St. Louis, MO, who through her weight loss journey developed a passion for fitness. She has taken that passion and created a blog website, Confessions of a Fit Girl, to help others achieve a healthy mind, body and spirit through exercise, nutrition and positivity.

www.confessionsofafitgirl.com

www.facebook.com/akamissj

www.jonelleboyd.com

It's Okay To Change Your Mind!

by Jennifer Urezzio

I'm sitting in the shower arguing with myself.

This happens more than you would think for someone who teaches, guides and supports consciousness. Here's what I'm saying: I don't want to write this! I Don't Want To Write This! I DON'T WANT TO WRITE THIS!! And now . . . I'm starting to cry. When someone with warrior energy cries, it can be very dramatic. I feel like being dramatic today.

What I don't want to do is write the piece for this book. Why? I don't believe I have anything to say to women. It annoys me. I get things down really quickly and this whole experience annoys me. I imagine women sharing relationship experiences that have the reader in tears – that's not me. I imagine women sharing stories that inspire the reader to take action – I'm kind of over doing that. On top of all of this, I'm annoyed at myself for sounding like a whiny crybaby (although these are not the words I use.)

Then it hits me ... or should I say I can finally hear what the Divine has been saying to me for days, weeks and months. It's okay to change your mind. It's okay to admit that you can't or don't want to do everything. It's okay to be vulnerable. Remember, Wonder Woman is a <u>fictional</u> character.

Once you have the awareness that it is okay to change your mind and you want to change the agreements you've made, well...then you have to take the hard step and rewrite those agreements. I realized that this article was only one manifestation of many experiences I have been saying yes to that may not have resonated with me the way I desired.

The first thing I decided I was going to stop saying yes to was feeling like I had to be the strongest person in the room to receive love, respect, money, etc. This really hit home recently during a conversation with my boyfriend, Warner, when he asked me why I didn't share with him that I was struggling with something. It was a difficult question to answer, and that was because I didn't want to appear weak or needy.

How can we allow anyone to support us if we are always playing superhero? We can't! The Divine supports us through human interaction and if we are not allowing that interaction, then guess what? We are not receiving all that we have been asking for from the Universe.

So, I created a strategy. I was going to practice the pause before every answer and every interaction. The PAUSE is this:

Someone asks me something. I pause … tune into my heart and Soul, and ask myself these questions: Do I really want to participate in this? What is my truth about this situation? What do I feel about this situation? What does my Soul want me to know about this situation?

It has been working and I'm feeling much more at peace with myself as well as feeling more profoundly supported by the Universe (and humans).

I guess what I want women to know is this: you are always changing. You have the right to do and be what is in alignment with your heart and Soul. AND, being vulnerable is the key to receiving what you desire.

About Jennifer Urezzio

Jennifer Urezzio is the founder of Soul Language and a master intuitive who uses her intuitive skills to help raise consciousness. Soul Language is a paradigm to put tangibility to Soul. She is the author of two books (available on Amazon): Soul Language Consciously Connecting To Your Soul for Success and A Little Book of Prayers. You can learn more at: www.soullanguage.us.

Creating a Sacred Practice That Works

Why do we need a sacred practice? When we feel separate from our higher power, that separation shows up in our lives as lack, pain, and suffering. Participating in a daily sacred practice that fits who you are will allow you to create in a more powerful way, feel more at peace, and know that you are safe no matter what challenge may appear in your experience.

http://www.soullanguage.us/sacredpractice/

The Art of Self Sabotage
by Elena Skyhawk

Have you ever wondered as a woman, how much we really sabotage ourselves? Where does this belief or pattern come from? Well as I have found out over the course of my life most of it comes from beliefs instilled in me as a child.

As a young girl growing up I was always told: *"be quiet; you're supposed to be seen, not heard."* And: *"Girls don't know what they're talking about."* Do these statements sound familiar? Do you feel your body resonating to what you think is true? They really are beliefs, and in most cases not even your beliefs. For me, some come from family members, especially the men; sometimes even mothers if they have taken on the beliefs of their husbands, brothers and fathers.

What does all of this have to do with self-sabotage? When I went to college my parents wouldn't pay for my schooling. The only reason women went to school was to get a "Mrs. degree," not to get something that was actually useful. That was still the prevalent thinking when I started college in 1978.

I'm a rebel and I kowtow to no one. Did I have boyfriends, of course I did, dated a lot and even fell in love a couple of times, but I also had a strong desire to be my own boss. To never allow others to dictate my thinking or what I was "supposed" to do.

Over time I started to believe what my boyfriends and others said; *"Just get a job, get married, have kids"*. Following their guidance, I sabotaged my dreams of becoming a veterinarian. While my friends graduated from vet school and launched their businesses, I was working for someone else at very little pay, all because I had been programmed by my parents to believe that girls weren't supposed to be independent.

Things finally started to turn around in my late twenties as I moved across the country to get away from family and start over my way. Funny thing is, if you don't change your beliefs and patterns they have a tendency to keep popping up. I went back to school and got an accounting degree and then a few years later a business degree and was on my way to starting a master's degree in marketing when I met my first metaphysical teacher. Boy was that an eye opener and for the first time in almost 30 years (ha-ha, I was only 30) I finally felt like I was being heard and understood. I realized it wasn't what was "out there" that mattered it was what was inside — really deep inside— that mattered.

So, what's a girl to do with this information? Jump on it and heal yourself so that you can go out and conquer the world? In a perfect world maybe, but in my world that's not exactly what happened. I would quickly move forward for a while, feeling really good about myself. I'd do some healing on myself, and then… wham! Something or someone from my old life would pop in and say hey that's not what you're supposed to be doing/saying/thinking. You name it they had all kinds of reasons. Foolishly I listened to them instead of the still small voice in my heart. I now understand that if we allow other's beliefs to override ours, believing everyone else knows better than we do, we will always be trapped in the self-sabotage cycle.

When you connect with your soul and realize what a phenomenal human being, greatly loved by Spirit, you really are, then self-sabotage can be released and you will start to heal.

This started to happen for me when I met my first mentor in 2000. He actually found me. That story is kind of hilarious, but I'll save it for another time. Serge was a shaman of Mohawk and Hawaiian heritage. He took me under his wing and taught me about shamanism and energy healing. He also explained who and what I was, yes I am a shaman, and yes it's a challenging path, but for me it's so fulfilling, full of love, forgiveness, wonderment and power.

I studied/worked with Serge for eight years until his passing in 2008. Today I carry on his teaching. I've incorporated a lot of what he taught into what I do. I became a minister and doctor of metaphysics. Now as a minister/shaman/healer/sage I help other's get out of their own way by finding the root cause of what's stopping them from moving forward.

Here's a great example of self-sabotage that I just recently fixed. Spirit has been telling me for several months to move my computer closer to the French doors in my living room so that I can get more natural light. I've found I love to do video's and live FB video, but where I had my computer (in the dining room) it just made it look so dark even with all the light I had on myself and the computer. I fought and fought and fought to not do it. Why? Good question…this is self-sabotage. You see, if I actually did what was suggested and it worked, once again it would mean Spirit knew better than my ego and horror of horrors I might actually get seen on the videos instead of always being in shadow. I finally made the move today and yep I was right, or should I say Spirit was right, the lighting over here is phenomenal, and I can actually be seen on the videos!

About Elena Skyhawk:

Elena Skyhawk has been gifted with claircognizance (clear knowing), and clairaudience (clear hearing). Over the years other clair's have made their appearance: clairsentient (clear feeling), clairvoyance (clear seeing).

Elena studied for several years with Serge "Runningwolf" Martel, a shaman of Mohawk/Hawaiian heritage.

Elena is a Shaman's Touch Healing Master/Teacher, and Reiki Master/Teacher. Elena is also a minister through I.M.M. (International Metaphysical Ministry) and holds a Doctoral Degree in Metaphysical Sciences through the University of Sedona.

She is working on the first of several shamanic books where she will be sharing the teachings she was given by Serge "RunningWolf" Martel.

http://www.spiritual-shaman.com

Using Sexual Polarity for Love and Business
By Tanja Diamond

My Dad was a powerful international businessman, I remember wanting to be just like him. But as a woman "doing" business like a man it can be a lonely journey. I'd like to share something I would do differently. Come on a journey of energetic power dynamics which once you understand and embrace will create thriving in your business and love life, instead of the mayhem I experienced early on.

Each gender has both masculine (yang) and feminine (yin) energies and we can either be a victim to them with our unwitting lack of awareness or harness them and become extraordinary.

Let me illustrate. I was dating this guy who wasn't moving in for a kiss after four weeks of dating. I asked him, are you attracted to me, yep he said he liked to take things slow. I was reading this book on sexual polarity and looking at myself I was decidedly running a TON of yang energy. I was into extreme sports, everyone I knew called me a serious badass (before it was popular), my reputation was formidable in everything I did. I decided to experiment a little on the next date.

I got into an outfit I didn't normally wear. I traded the jeans and combat boots for a dress, though I kept the combat boots. My date came to the door, I took some deep breaths and slowed down, I thought of sensuous dancing and let my body relax and soften.

I was stunned at his response right away. It wasn't the dress, it was the shift I felt from him. I waited at the car door instead of racing out and jumping in, I didn't suggest where to go, I asked him where he was taking me. I kept deepening into the idea of softening. Fifteen minutes into the drive I was fascinated by his posture change, he seemed "fuller". He told me he wasn't sure what was going on, but he felt turned on and was inspired by our experience. I did get kissed that night.

This is the power of the sexual polarity inherent in everything we do and every person we're in contact with. Understanding this has impacted everything in my life.

If I'm in same energetic dynamic with a man, my yang to his yang, it creates competition or if he's conflict avoidant, moves him to his yin aspect. Knowing this helps me build rapport and influence. When interacting with women, if a woman is in her yin, I meet her there with just a hint of masculine edge. If she's in her yang I can soften, or up her, but not meet her in sync or we'll feel like we're on the battlefield.

Women in business run a lot of yang energy, especially if they have kids and a household to handle. It's the get it done attitude, managing, focus, action, with little time for dreaming and sensuality. And although I'm writing this in hetero speak the same energetic ideas are in place no matter the gender.

In love relationships women want their men to be the man, yet most men will become yin instead of try and out masculine their women if they love them. This makes the woman unhappy and even more yang and "demanding" of how he man up. It's a bad scene, no one is happy, and the relationship will break.

I thought I was better in business in yang mode. I thought being in my yin meant being weak and lacking power. I was wrong. I find that being able to swing from being task driven to creative in a breath, flowing easily from work mode to lover mode, I'm in the best of all places. From the analytic to the creative, checking in with both, allows the wisdom of each to lead me. Intuition and action side by side. My decisions happen faster knowing that they are in alignment with all of me, my heart and head. If you find yourself too yin and struggle with structure and format, or don't get taken as seriously by men you can change that dynamic too.

Start the change by first, becoming aware of the energy, yin or yang, you're carrying most of the time and your body tension. We can't change what we don't see, so get aware. Lots of Yang feels hard, driven, tension in the jaw, neck and shoulders, higher desire to release sexual energy in a hurry, more aggressive feeling. Yin feels softer, more distracted, creative desire, from the heart and flowy. Tension would be in the abdomen and pelvis, but the energy would be more about slowing down and feeling, than trying to push it out. You may even shut down sexually.

Now see if you can bring more of the opposite to you...even if you have to get silly, dress up, play, over exaggerate if you need to. If you want more yang, stride around the house, act "manly", sit wide, scratch your balls, ask for a beer. If you want more yin, dance softly, hum, get wispy, speak softly, slower, act like a southern belle. Stand a little sideways to someone you're talking to instead of squared off. Tilt your head to the side just a tad, relax your lips and watch what happens with the other person.

Soon you will be able to walk into a boardroom of all good old boys and with a simple gesture have their undivided attention, and then shift that into utter respect. And you will engage your lover deeply and be deeply enriched from that too. You get the idea. Cultivate both aspects, get and stay curious. This play will help you feel into each part, so you can learn to incorporate it during your days. Eventually you can feel which energy to bring and go there with a breath, now that's power!

About Tanja Diamond

Tanja Diamond creator of the technology of Modern Tantra –The Six Foundations of Integrated Living and High Speed Evolution guides her clients to Their PERSONAL FREEDOM by integrating knowledge into their entire beings and teaching them the Art of Insourcing–a place of their most conscious and true self. She calls it Integrated Intelligence.

Through Tanja's work and personal journey, she has unlocked the code of our evolutionary design, expanding the limits of human potential which enables her clients to go beyond the norm, indeed go beyond even success to a place of extraordinary called Peak Arousal Living

Gift

Thanks for taking the time to be here with us and I have an exclusive discounted offer just for you. Your Life Unleashed Video Masterclass. Discover the unique 5 minute practices designed to transport you to your happiness and Personal Freedom.

http://bit.ly/2AVy0G0

The Power Within
by Debe Bloom

I'm a twin. I was born the younger of the two, which made me the baby of the family of 4. We have two older brothers; but, I'm the youngest. We are one of the lucky ones: We were raised in a very loving home. It was amazing growing up with a twin sister: I always had a friend and someone to do things with....-- playing "Barbie's in our playroom, climbing the neighbors' fences, going on our first date. From being just the two of us, it eventually became the four of us with our spouses and then our families. Losing our parents was a huge setback for all of us, but I drew strength from my twin as she always protected me. Always.

Life went on. My first marriage didn't work out very well, but my twin was always by my side supporting me and understanding me. When the marriage came to a halt, initiated by me, my sister propped me up and made sure I wouldn't fall down, emotionally, financially, spiritually. Always by my side. She encouraged my inner strength to evolve.

I met another man. He became my knight in shining armor. He was kind, sweet, and he listened to me when I spoke. He spent time with my twin, which won me over, because he appreciated her as the wonderful woman she offered. And, he supported me, lifted me up and understood my agony when cancer laced itself around my twin's inside and eventually took her breath away. My husband was my pillar.

We grew together as a unit, deep in our friendship foundation and entwined in our romantic side. I was blind to most his shortcomings and accepted him and what I perceived as all his faults in our life. Day after day, year after year; I accepted him; I trusted him; I allowed him to live his life and I would follow...until.

Until one day in the very recent past, I could no longer 'accept'; I could no longer close my eyes and let him continue to destroy what we had together by denying that he was an alcoholic. I drew the line. I mean "THE" line...not the lines I had drawn before ---the ones that I wasn't strong enough to mean or frankly care about enough to fight for; the ones that there was no follow-up. This time, I spoke up with a vengeance and gave him that famous ultimatum: you admit you're an alcoholic and get some help or "just get out". I spoke those words knowing he wouldn't leave. I spoke those words because my safety and the safety of our children provided me the inner strength to finally speak up on this subject. His hurt feelings were not of a concern any longer.

I'm so proud of him. He hasn't had a touch of alcohol since that day. He has joined AA, gotten a sponsor, obtained a therapist. I've joined him in therapy because two minds are better than one, especially if they live together. In reality, I was going because I was asked to come and support his efforts and I am all about doing whatever I can to support him in this new journey. 'Maybe it's the alcoholism that has been keeping his hugs and kind gestures away from me....maybe we can find a solve'. That was my thought.

What we found, was not really a solve...not yet...we found him running away from me. During a session, he announced that he wanted a separation from me. Blindsided me completely. Twenty-four hours after that the separation, it turned into a divorce and he moved out, lock, stock and barrel. That was not propelled by me in any fashion: he actually chose to go to a motel to 'think clearer' that first night. "Whatever you need to do to find your way, I totally support you" bit me in the butt.

There's a good ending to this story. We started communicating like we have never talked before and less than a month later, he moved back in. We are definitely a work in progress. And it's hard; it's very hard.

But those 4 weeks that he was gone, I had to muster up all the inner strength that was lying dormant inside of me. Without fear, without embarrassment and without hesitation, I called upon my tribe (my family and my friends) to help me, and they were there without a second thought. The phone calls, the visits, the text messages...all supporting me, lifting me up. Some were putting some wicked thoughts into my head, some were being incredibly 'soft' for what he was going through. All were giving me food for thought and allowing me to go deep within myself and choose my own truth; choose our own truth.

I will be able to forgive my husband for his running from our marriage, but the pain in my heart will take time to heal. I am blessed to have a group of people who care and love me and support me. I am amazed and surprised what level of strength was lying dormant for so many years. Maybe this shake-up in our marriage was a godsend albeit the pain that I have endured.

I question myself if living with the years of pain and feeling slighted, the lies and coverups, the risk of my safety and that of our children was equal to o' maybe even more than the "recent four weeks" when I realized the power I ha l within to be able to come out the other side of this episode being stronger, being more aware, being a deeper me.

About Debe Bloom

Debe Bloom resides in Ventura County, enjoys being a mobile entrepreneur with her husband (www.DebeAndRick.com) and a Notary Public & Signing Agent. She is a member of Women in Technology, National Association of Female Executives, among other organizations and was awarded the Women Entrepreneur Business Award of Excellence in 2011 and volunteers in community activities.

Epilogue

What surprised me most as I read the stories submitted for this eBook was that they were nothing that I expected, and yet everything I expected. Although I kept the universe completely open to allow what each person wanted to write, in the back of my mind I had ideas when I created the title! LOL.

The surprise was the sense of seriousness, almost darkness, that many women chose to share. Coming through it and recognizing their journey in it was key to truly find a balanced, thriving life. Each woman shared what they learned to LIVE fully and completely. Which is exactly what I expected. And therefore, they thrive.

There is also love, light even humor as they share the importance of their story. Through the seriousness, there are also powerful lessons from simple things in life, like mom's chair, ice cream, a tomato and even my garden.

The one driving message of this book? Your path to living an unstoppable thriving life is a twisting, turning journey. Ultimately, it's about your creating conscious connection as to what is happening in your life right now. It is realizing that this journey is making the woman you are meant to be. And with each twist along the road, you will evolve into a better version of her as you're feeling power to choose, know who you are, change your mindset, clarify expectations of self and others, and define your own success.

Stories intertwine us. They are the fiber and history of who we are. Keep telling stories. They heal, inspire and transform lives!

One thing all these women storytellers will tell you is how open they are to connect! Don't be afraid to join us! Also, I believe you have a story to share. More Unscripted Stories eBooks are coming, and I invite you to become an author and leave your legacy for another!

Learn more here: http://www.unscriptedstories.com/become-an-author/

Not sure what to share yet feel called to be a part? Contact me! I can usually figure it out with a quick chat!

With love,

Ann M. Evanston

79106917R00133

Made in the USA
San Bernardino, CA
11 June 2018